CONSTITUTIONAL COURTS
OF THE
UNITED STATES

CONSTITUTIONAL COURTS OF THE UNITED STATES

The Formal and Informal Relationships between the District Courts, the Courts of Appeals, and the Supreme Court of the U.S.

Stephen T. Early, Jr.

GEORGE MASON UNIVERSITY

1977

LITTLEFIELD, ADAMS & CO.
Totowa, New Jersey

Library of Congress Cataloging in Publication Data

Early, Stephen Tyree, 1923-
    Constitutional Courts of the United States.

    (A Littlefield, Adams quality paperback; no. 320)
    Includes bibliographical references and index.
    1. United States. Supreme Court. 2. United States.
Courts of Appeals. 3. United States. District Courts.
I. Title.
KF8700.E2   347'.73'1   76-44501
ISBN 0-8226-0320-9

PRINTED IN THE UNITED STATES OF AMERICA

Contents

Preface

This book is designed to provide a realistic overview of the federal court system of the United States. I intend neither to attack nor to defend the status quo in the national constitutional courts here, nor do I offer a blueprint for the reform of the judiciary. What I aim to show, in practice as well as in theory, is how our system of national justice operates in the District Courts, the Courts of Appeals, and the Supreme Court, and how these levels interact with one another.

What emerges from this study is that the federal courts do not form a single, cohesive, centrally directed system, all parts of which function in synchrony. While the courts are related to each other, they rarely all act in concert. This book explores not only the ways in which the national court system works as a system, but also the ways in which its components maintain some autonomy.

The relation between the components has two dimensions, the institutional and the human. The institutional features include the number and types of courts, their general and particular jurisdictions, their procedural rules, their functions, and their officers. Probably because these features are accessible, manageable, visible, and reasonably precise, they are the ones that have received the most attention. Admittedly, they are necessary for an understanding of the legal system, and they are recognized throughout this book. A brief and nontechnical outline of them is provided in Chapter 2 for those whose knowledge needs to be refreshed. A reader who wishes to delve further into these phases of intercourt relations as controlled by the details of national jurisdiction and procedures can find ample material in any law library.[1]

Taken by itself, however, the institutional framework is not enough for a thorough understanding of how the courts work. The informal and human aspects are also extremely important. Fortunately, increasing attention is being paid to them. From the scholarly end of the legal profession have come the thoughts of Roscoe Pound, Benjamin Cardozo, Oliver Wendell Holmes, Jr., and Learned Hand. More recently and largely from outside the legal fraternity have come analyses by John Schmidhauser, Kenneth Vines, Sydney Ulmer, Glendon Schubert, Walter Murphy, and a host of other commentators. All agree that the judicial system must be conceived of as a human system, one in which the parts are activated, directed—and sometimes subverted—by ordinary mortals (albeit ones who have a specialized learning that has admitted them to the inner sanctum of social control and conflict resolution). Nominally, at least, they play their roles in the judicial system according to strict application of clearly defined parameters, and, in fact, the system does largely stay within its formal bounds. But the human element colors its processes and determines its ultimate product in myriad subtle ways not suggested by the formal externalities. This book strives to convey understanding not only of the formal but also of the informal aspects of judicial operation.

The subject is not easy to deal with. Except for such work as

1. Readily available are controlling statutes, rules of civil and criminal procedure, and local rules of the courts. The now dated but still useful book by F. Frankfurter and J. W. Landis, *The Business of the Supreme Court: A Study of the Federal Judicial System* (Macmillan, 1928) and the more current study by E. Gressman and R. L. Stern, *Supreme Court Practice*, 4th ed. (Bureau of National Affairs, 1969) are indispensable tools of reference. In addition, the student will find helpful the *Annual Report of the Director, Administrative Office of the United States Courts* (Government Printing Office); H. G. Finns, *Federal Jurisdiction and Procedure* (Bobbs-Merrill, 1960); H. M. Hart, Jr., and Herbert Wechsler, *The Judicial Code and Rules of Procedure in the Federal Courts* (Foundation Press, 1954); H. J. Friendly, *Federal Jurisdiction: A General View* (Columbia University Press, 1973); G. H. Webb and T. C. Bianco, *Federal Jurisdiction and Federal Procedure* (Holt, Rinehart & Winston, 1970); and T. Schussler, *Federal Courts: Jurisdiction and Practice* (Gould, 1967).

that of Professors W. F. Murphy, Kenneth Vines, Herbert Jacob, Joel Grossman, and a few others, the lower courts of the constitutional system have received relatively little attention. Little data about them other than that published by official sources are available, and much of the analysis directed at their decision-making processes, roles, personnel, and institutional character has been of particular tribunals. For instance, the Court of Appeals, Fifth Circuit, has been a favorite object of attention because of the prominence attained by it during the civil rights struggles of the 1950's and 1960's. And much of the effort made to date has been directed to structural or technical features of the lower-court system. Inquiry into most aspects of the judiciary and judicial processes is made yet more difficult by the large number of inferior courts and judges and by their spatial dispersion.

But perhaps the most chilling deterrent to analysis is the fact, immediately encountered by the inquirer, that the national judiciary is much like a baronial fiefdom held under constitutional grant. Its layered feudal elite seem determined to maintain their silence about the nature, business, processes, and ethics of their realm. With rare exceptions, willing communication is not a principal attribute of its membership. It is as though intuition, if not agreement, had led all to stay mute in order that the force of judiciary mysteries (on which public respect and acceptance in part rest) should not be dissipated by analysis and revelation.

Hence, what follows relies heavily on the episodic researches of a few scholars who have focused mainly upon either formal aspects of the judicial system or upon ascertainable personal data, little of which is about lower-court personnel and performance. Insights, clues, and suspicions have also come from public utterances of judicial personnel (largely but not wholly by Justices), judicial biographies, and a few years of following the judicial process. Using these means I have tried to identify and understand both the principal integrative and the principal centrifugal factors operating among the constitutional courts and judges of the United States.

There is, of course, an infinite number of relationships between the inferior courts and the Supreme Court. It has been impossible to identify all of them or to examine exhaustively all facets of those subjects attended to. For example, we must leave unexplored the role of discretion exercised by law-enforcement personnel while they are arresting and investigating;

by public prosecutors when they are negotiating a plea bargain, fixing a charge, or abandoning a case; or by judges when they are building a trial record or imposing sentence—even though questionable exercise of discretion has laid the foundation for more than one case for High Court review. Yet, in a very pragmatic sense, everything that enters into the adjudicatory process—even the fact that plaintiff A was only able to retain attorney B instead of the more experienced attorney C—will leave some mark upon its operation and thereby upon inter-court relations as well.

In consequence, only those aspects have been identified and considered that are thought to be most important because most influential, most widespread, or most visible. The reader may easily think of others not referred to, or of nuances not mentioned, but the coverage here does not purport to turn over every stone. In the interest of reasonable brevity, the inquiry that follows sets out a minimum number of illustrations, avoids detailed analysis of procedural matters, and tries to make clear the dominant patterns of interaction among courts, with more emphasis being given to informal features than to technical matters of structure, rules, and procedures.

I make public acknowledgment of my debt to those who made indispensable contributions to this project. To Professors Barbara Knight (George Mason University), George W. Spicer (Emeritus, University of Virginia) and Robert J. Steamer (University of Massachusetts, Boston) go my most grateful thanks for their close reading of these pages and for their many helpful suggestions. To Mrs. Gloria Jones and Mrs. Virginia Swain go my appreciation for the typing of these chapters. And to Ms. Pat White, copy editor, who caught more errors of style and organization than I like to admit to creating, goes full credit for her professional contribution. Of course all responsibility for errors of omission or commission is exclusively mine.

S. T. E.

CONSTITUTIONAL COURTS
OF THE
UNITED STATES

CHAPTER 1

The System of National Courts

ESTABLISHMENT OF THE SYSTEM

The distribution of judicial power in the United States has been a problem since the days of the creation and first implementation of the Constitution. Its framers had two choices. On the one hand, they could leave all adjudication arising under national laws to the courts of the several states, with the possibility of review by a single national appellate court. Alternatively, they could provide for the creation of a separate system of national courts having independent jurisdiction bestowed on them by the new plan of government.

What emerged from the deliberations was a compromise. In Article III, the Convention merely defined the types of cases and controversies to which the judicial power of the United States might extend. It mandated the existence of a single national Supreme Court. It gave Congress discretion to establish unspecified courts subordinate to the Supreme Court, and it ensured the objectivity of decisions by insulating judges from pressures emanating from the political branches. The Convention's clear preference for an independent national judiciary, however, seems to be implied in its empowering Congress to create subordinate courts and in its designation of the types of cases such courts might try.

Various reasons were advanced for following this course of action. Many of the arguments reflected the distrust the states felt toward the new general government, for the tides of localism ran strong in that era. During the time of the Confederation and for decades after the Constitution was adopted, many persons regarded the states as the jurisdictions of government to which they owed their first and superior allegiance.

Also, the existence of a separate system of national lower courts would enable the national government to protect itself and to enforce its own laws through its own agencies. Actions that threatened to destroy the administration of its laws by undermining their authority (or that of the agencies which administered them, or of the governmental system on which the existence of a judiciary depended) might be punished independently of the "let or hindrance" of the states. If unpunished, offenses such as treason, espionage, sedition, bribery of federal officers or employees, interference with the performance of national governmental functions, obstruction of recruiting efforts for the military forces, fraud under the revenue statutes, and destruction of federal property would weaken and might ultimately destroy the authority and perhaps the existence of the national government by holding its competence, prestige, and status up to contempt, and by revealing its impotence to punish those who would subvert it.

Some actions under the Constitution, laws, and treaties of the United States, it was argued, ought not be left to state courts. Suits involving diplomatic representatives sent to the United States by foreign governments, suits arising under international law, suits between two or more states, suits against the United States, and suits between the United States and a state were not appropriate for settlement by state judicial authority. The diversity of interpretation that would stem from such an arrangement was also thought to be sound reason for permitting the establishment of an independent national judiciary, should Congress in the future feel it expedient to bring one into being. The initial implementation of the Constitution's delegation of congressional authority to "constitute tribunals inferior to the Supreme Court" came with the Judiciary Act of 1789 and has been the basis of many later enactments.[1]

Virtually all statutes pertaining to the judiciary of the United

1. The impact of political forces upon the establishment of the new judicial system and upon subsequent modifications thereto is treated in R. J. Richardson and K. Vines, *The Politics of Federal Courts* (Little, Brown, 1970), ch. 2.

States have represented attacks upon the single problem of how to provide a system of national courts adequate to the size of the country and appropriate to its federal form of government. The problem does not lend itself to a single final solution, and therefore, it has not yet been fully solved. For the most part, efforts to deal with it have been experimental, piecemeal, *ad hoc*, and sometimes influenced by forces outside the judicial system. Various combinations of features have been tried, only to be modified or abandoned.

UNITY VERSUS AUTONOMY

Both political theories and geography have influenced the development of the judiciary. In providing for a system of lower national courts the realities of political life have made it necessary to accommodate the strong strain of localism inherent in and vital to American federalism. From the beginning of its history, national versus local considerations have weighed heavily in the development of the constitutional court system as have other, less fundamental and more petty, demands. At the same time, the great expanse of the nation has worked for the creation and preservation of a spatially decentralized system of national courts. Politics, party, patronage, and local autonomy have been powerful agents of our national growth, and all four have been, and in varying degrees remain, ingredients of our national judiciary.

The autonomy of individual national tribunals is only partially diminished by the extent to which they are integrated into the judicial structure, which in fact is partly centralized. Their position in the national system of judicial administration is clearly more a subordination of tribunals than it is of judges, more formal than operational. Today, lower constitutional courts are coordinated, but not tightly and hierarchically integrated, for the judges of the different tribunals are not all members of a single national court, subject to one superior and transferable from one tribunal to another as needed. Although there are linkages between them—some vertical between levels of courts, others horizontal, joining courts within a level of the structure —the courts within each level retain, from one another and from those above, great independence of action and an almost uncompromised identity as autonomous operating entities.

In another dimension, judicial autonomy is represented by the constitutional guarantees of independence, by the assurance of an irreducible salary and tenure during "good behavior," and by the setting of the judicial apart from the legislative and executive branches according to Montesquieu's formula for liberty. Such guarantees, however, protect inferior-court judges only against coercion by Congress and the executive. They do not protect them, especially district judges, from the desire to be liked socially and to be professionally respected and approved by their peers, especially those whose outlooks, values, interests, backgrounds, preferences, biases, and associations are congenial to their own.

There is a connected pattern in the way the skills and energies of approximately five hundred federal judges, possessing different degrees and kinds of competence, are deployed over a continent-wide area, but within the vast territory served by the judicial system there are also discernible differences of local conditions, manners, and economic activity. Parochial forces operate around, on and through a District Court and may be so strong that, as in some civil rights cases in the South, even the Department of Justice on occasion can be reluctant in jury trials to use lawyers from outside the area. (When it was necessary to do so, the Department was careful to use counsel whose background and speech identified them with the locality.) The extent to which the lower federal courts possess either formal or actual autonomy of action facilitates their accommodation of local conditions to the less flexible features of the judicial process.

The autonomy and number of inferior judges produce some difficulties for the easy administration of justice. Among lower courts a considerable variation in administrative standards exists —enough to inconvenience litigants and dismay practicing attorneys and students of the federal judiciary. Also, the multiplicity of lower courts and their traditional independence in internal operation inhibit reform and the spread of new administrative techniques.

Lower courts have their vested interests to protect: their institutional identities, their external constituencies and defenders, their purposes and values, their sense of status, their relationships of authority and deference, and their symbols and operational environment. But the roots of their "bureaucratic" responses to higher authority are sunk deeply in the fertile soil of legal formality and judicial professionalism and are watered by the fine points of methodology, procedure, structure, jurisdiction, and relationship built into the existing judicial system.

THE LOWER COURTS

The Roles of the Lower Courts. The District Courts, and, to a lesser degree, the Courts of Appeals, bring down to a local level the authority of the national law, enhancing its effectiveness while demonstrating its strengths and weaknesses. In those cases raising constitutional questions, the continuing vitality of the fundamental law is also brought down to the operating level of individual controversy. The inferior tribunals are intermediate agents in the initiation and refining of public policy, effecting exertions of authority both immediate and remote in relation to the litigants' interests. These courts provide plaintiffs in suitable circumstances a choice of judicial systems to which to bring their appeal to law. Within the limited relationship between the state and national systems, they offer some prospect that conflicting legal rights and obligations defined under national authority can be adjusted by national courts, and that problems of a social and economic character that cannot be relieved by resort to the political process may be successfully converted into legal disputes suitable for adjudication.

The need for lower national courts to protect national authority is no longer as great as it was during the initial decades of government under the Constitution. Such courts nevertheless continue to bring the sovereign authority of the national government closer to the daily affairs, the respect, and the comprehension of the people. Because a separate system of national courts exists, rights created under, and offenses committed against, the authority of national law do not have to compete for attention in the same courts as those arising under state and local law.[2] The existence of a separate system of

2. Congress has left to state courts enforcement of some non-criminal rights of action created by national statutes, in effect making the state courts tribunals vested with "the judicial power of the United States." Its competence to require state courts to enforce rights of action created by national law is established beyond doubt. See *Testa* v. *Katt*, 330 U.S. 386 (1947). Congress has authorized use of state courts for perfection of rights arising under the Fugitive Slave Laws, the Emergency Price Control Act, the Fair Labor Standards Act, and the Securities and Exchange Act, among others. For further treatment of the subject see L. Mayers, *The American Legal System* (Harper & Row, 1964), pp. 196–198.

national district and appellate courts provides national laws
with national tribunals supposedly having a national point of
view, dedicated to national interests and values under the
Constitution, laws, and treaties of the United States and to the
service of national objectives. These courts increase opportunities for the development of judicial specialization in areas
of law having a vital relationship to national well-being. And,
perhaps most important, they eliminate the need to accommodate prosecutions arising under national authority and the
protection of national interests to the existence of fifty different
state systems of judicial procedure. The inferior trial and
appellate courts of the national judicial system provide a
reasonably efficient safeguard against local interference with, or
nullification of, national law by local authorities and local
courts.

The Practical Outlook of the Lower Courts.   In this, as in
most other areas of government activity touching the federal
relationship, the evaluation of observed or anticipated practical
consequences has provided the judiciary a measure by which
constitutional doctrine has been worked out and applied
pragmatically, conventionally, and conveniently. The bulk of
litigation that comes to the lower federal courts enables them
to steer clear of abstractions and broad theoretical generaliza-
tions. Most litigants before the lower tribunals want practical
answers to practical problems, not theoretical disquisitions on
matters of abstract principle. Yet these same courts are the
ones into which the NAACP, NAM, AFL-CIO, and ACLU, as
well as individual plaintiffs, sometimes bring innovative arguments that persuade trial-court judges to enunciate new constitutional principle and to set, temporarily at least, new social
policy. The vagaries of the appellate process determine whether
such decisions achieve permanent status. Withal, the course of
lower national courts has long been one of cautious reliance
upon judgments of experience rather than on those of specula-
tion. Adherence to the "case or controversy" rule; the avoidance
of moot, academic, and hypothetical questions and of advisory

---

Moreover, the Supremacy Clause of the Constitution says that state
courts cannot refuse to enforce federal statutory rights when they are
contrary to local policy. This is true even when the national statute is
penal—at least where the state courts under state law have jurisdiction
appropriate and sufficient to adjudicate the controversy.

opinions; and the cautious employment of declaratory judgments all testify to the reluctance of trial and lower appellate courts to indulge in theoretical decision-making apart from the specific situations of fact at hand.

This emphasis upon pragmatic tests plays into the hands of the lower courts. It magnifies their significance as builders of trial records and determiners of fact in close contact with local values and interests. Their propensity is to keep the application of constitutional principles and statutory mandates meaningfully attuned to the realities of modern life. Hence, the adage that the "Constitution is what the Supreme Court say it is" must be qualified by recognizing that it is the trial and intermediate courts that give life to law by applying it to the settlement of disputes. Just as other actors in the process of governance are affected by determinations of the Supreme Court, the Supreme Court is affected by lower-court attitudes toward, and compliance with, its determinations. A decision by the High Court is more final, but has little more vitality than the lower courts are willing to give it.

A primary function of the lower courts is to make national law practical. In sharp contrast, the Supreme Court tries to preserve at least a semblance of uniformity by eliminating the most disruptive aberrations from national law, by ironing out conflicts between authorities of equal rank below, and in general by serving as moderator of the national judicial and legal systems. The High Court performs this, one of its most useful functions, to the extent that it controls the shortsightedness or parochialism that sometimes colors lower-court business.[3] In the last analysis, however, fulfillment of these supervisory roles seems to depend more on the lower tribunals' voluntary disciplined acceptance of their subordinate but semiautonomous positions than it does upon the preeminent formal position of and exercise of supervisory authority by the Supreme Court.

THE SUPREME COURT

Its Two Images. The Supreme Court has acquired in the course of time a dual image. One is the image of public

3. See Paul Freund, "Review and Federalism," in Edmond Cahn, ed., *Supreme Court and Supreme Law* (Bloomington: Indiana University Press, 1954).

expectation, of civics books and Independence Day oratory. This is the Court that holds the Union together, harmonizes relations between the branches of government, protects civil rights and liberties, and safeguards the rights of persons and property. This is the Court that educates the American people in the values of the Constitution, refurbishing these ideals constantly in an effort to make them for succeeding generations of Americans, each increasingly removed from the heritage of 1776, as bright as they were during the founding era. This is the Court that keeps the nation's conscience, that answers the big questions of a fundamental character. This is the Court at the pinnacle of a three-tiered judicial structure, maintaining symmetry in the body of national law and exercising supervision over the inferior tribunals' conduct of business.

These functions are part of the Court's role in the constitutional scheme of things, but they are the consequence of special features. The "big questions" of constitutional law raising basic issues of public policy have frequently grown out of test cases —cases carefully prepared to present precisely the right question framed in the way most apt to elicit the desired answer. A notable new legal principle occasionally evolves from what was initially only a casual bit of litigation, but most cases for which Supreme Court review is vainly sought begin and remain casual litigation, important only to their parties. Suits presenting the Court with questions of law which are only that or but little more do not provide the Court with occasions to make sweeping determinations of broad constitutional principle out of which so much of its supporting mythology springs.

The second image is of the Court as a working body. The Supreme Court's business has a dull, almost mechanical side, a less familiar and less gaudy dimension. The Court is a court of law. It cannot use its broad discretionary jurisdiction to shield itself completely from narrow, conventional matters. It still expends much of its time and energy responding to questions that are federal in nature but that ought not command the attention of the nation's highest tribunal. The Court has been criticized because it has accepted insignificant, prosaic cases from lower courts and, having done so, has proceeded to a decision instead of dismissing them. It has failed to establish a sound and clear working guide for granting appeal or review by certiorari petition. That failure is said to encourage attorneys who are occupied with an immediate case, focused on a client's interests, and perhaps under pressure from the client, unwisely to seek review when by any reasonable standard no basis for it exists.

Distinctive Features of the Supreme Court. But is the Supreme Court merely another court of law superimposed on the working trial and intermediate appellate tribunals? It would be more helpful, perhaps, to ask whether or not the Supreme Court is different from the other courts of the regular constitutional system and, if it is different, how.

Certainly, as numerous commentators have pointed out, the Justices, like their counterparts in lower courts, have been trained in the system of case law to reason by analogy and to respect the force of precedent in the common-law tradition. But whereas the forms of that tradition and the training it requires are preserved in the procedures and formalisms of Supreme Court operations, Justice Frankfurter, for one, has conceded that they did not help him come to grips with the details of day-to-day decision-making as a member of the High Court.[4] Those traditions and the training that accompanies them provide a blueprint and a toolkit for constructing standards of policy enunciated as judge-made case law, but questions of private law which figure so prominently in the work of lower courts, in the common law, and in legal training are virtually absent from the work of the Supreme Court.

Frankfurter's message implies that the High Court is not *merely* another court of law. Rather, the Supreme Court is primarily a *public-law* court making a continuing exegesis of the fundamental law, construing the meaning of public statutes, and regulating the interrelationships of a citizenry and its government. The Supreme Court is occupied chiefly with statutory and constitutional construction and with politics, not with correcting lower-court error or assuring justice for individuals.

The ease and convenience of ignoring the differences between the United States Supreme Court and other tribunals, state and national, has probably greatly obscured the nature of the institution, what it does, the values it serves, and its proper role in American life and government. In discharging their role before

---

4. F. Frankfurter, "Some Observations on the Nature of the Judicial Process of Supreme Court Litigation," 98 *Proceedings of the American Philosophical Society* 233 (1954), at p. 238. See also Frankfurter, "The Supreme Court in the Mirror of Justices," 105 *University of Pennsylvania Law Review* 781 (1957).

the High Tribunal, lawyers find it both necessary and convenient to perpetuate use of the traditional forms and methods of their craft. Until recently, students of political science rarely studied the Supreme Court except through its product analyzed as case law, and even today most law schools continue this approach. (Nevertheless, nowadays for both groups instruction in the human and political features of the judicial process is displacing or taking position beside the older way.)

Moreover, there is as yet no consistently worked-out conceptualization of the Supreme Court's nature and role in the governmental system. There is no schema that acknowledges the Court's relationship to the decision-making of other units and branches of government at all levels. There is none that incorporates the impact of pressure-group activity and other forms of political power upon the policy-making and decisional processes of the judiciary. And there is none that explains adequately how decisions are made—not as matters of briefs, arguments, conferences, or other institutionalized procedures, but as products of judicial intellectualization. How does a judge or Justice assign weight to facts presented for his consideration? Why may the same fact be regarded as immaterial by one Justice but as material and determinative by a colleague voting on the same case? How are conflicts between competing values, each presenting a legitimate and equal claim to recognition, resolved in the mind of a Justice? Given the high level of abstraction characteristic of many statutory phrases and of virtually all constitutional phrases of judicial significance, how does a Justice balance the interests at stake when public authority endeavors to restrain individual freedom?

It may even be appropriate to ask whether, to a preponderant degree, questions such as these *are* or *can* really be resolved by investigation and deliberation. Perhaps the "judgment intuitive" is more often recorded in the pages of the *United States Reports* than is ordinarily suspected, camouflaged as judgments are by the *stare decisis* tradition. Once one begins to ask these and allied questions about what it is that the Supreme Court does and how the Justices go about performing their functions, the inadequacy, the lifeless artificiality, of the more traditional explanations of and attitudes toward the judicial process become apparent. In the same vein, Morris R. Cohen concluded twenty-five years ago that we can no longer regard the Supreme Court as merely a law court. The cases which come to it involve determinations of complex and varied facts, the results produced by those facts, and values often competing for acceptance. The questions brought to it are political, social, and economic and, unless law is accepted as embracing all social knowledge, are beyond the training of judges to solve.[5]

What other court in the United States can through its decisions play such a central role in bringing about a national realignment of racial and other minorities? What other court can reconstruct the representative character of our legislatures, state and national? Or make of the power to tax for the support of government a many-faceted device for achieving more complete social justice? Or redefine according to twentieth-century standards the relationship of religion and public power? Or determine the substantive answers to many other of the most fundamental, complex, and troubling social and economic problems of the nation? Neither an inferior district nor appellate court could accomplish such ends.

Two qualifications must be advanced at this point. First: as a court of law the High Court probably cannot ever escape the traditional institutional framework within which lawyers and courts function in the United States. Further, there seems to be no reason why it should. The significant fact is that the Supreme Court is "a very special kind of court."[6] Full appreciation of its unique characteristics may have been part of the reason why Justice Felix Frankfurter also held to the opinion that "Judicial service as such has no significant relationship to the kinds of litigation that come before the Supreme Court, to the types of issues they raise, to the qualities that these actualities require for wise decision."[7]

The second qualification is that no claim is made that the Supreme Court is the only regular constitutional court concerned with or involved in policy-making or with the relationship of policy-making to the processes of governance. Whatever the court may be, public policy in its broadest sense is embodied in the issue of every case decided and the law applied to every case's resolution. This is true of a question of private law, such as title to an automobile, as well as of a question of constitutional law.

5. *Reason and Law* (Glencoe, Ill.: Free Press, 1950), pp. 73–74.
6. F. Frankfurter, "The Supreme Court in the Mirror of Justices," 105 *University of Pennsylvania Law Review* 781 (1957), at p. 785.
7. Ibid.

The Supreme Court's Teleological Orientation. The work of the Supreme Court has about it a prospective and teleological character largely absent from the work of the lower courts. Even today lower-court work remains overwhelmingly retrospective and mechanistic,[8] and only rarely does it permit decisions with a forward-looking quality. Litigation before the High Court, however, often involves questions of constitutional interpretation and adjudication. Such issues present obvious and strong opportunities for anticipatory decision-making, for it is then that the objectives of constitutional construction and the urgings of interests seeking preferential recognition look at the future and seek to identify with conceptions of the "higher good" and the "forward" development of public policy.

When the Justices tackle the more controversial issues before the country they are most apt to reveal the direction of their purposiveness and their retrospective or prospective attitudes. The teleological character of the Justices' decisions is often obscured by judicial conditioning and the traditionalism of their profession, which impels them to show at least the appearance of conformity to the rule of precedent and to the other conserving features of law and judicial procedure. But the Justices' readiness to ignore or to reverse precedent strongly implies that their reliance upon it is not the result of a binding duty.

A reading of the *United States Reports* shows that precedent (otherwise called the "intentions" of the Constitution's framers, or the "original meaning" of its language, or whatever other authority is evoked in order to show established constitutional doctrine) is but one of many factors in constitutional decision-making. While they profess to look back to first principles, the Justices have shown an unmistakable willingness to anticipate the practical consequences of decisions.[9] The record leaves no doubt that Justices from John Marshall to the present have been as interested in the anticipated results of their decisions as they have been in adhering to pre-existing principles or judge-made rules. Today, arguments based on the alternative policy choices open to the Justices as measured by practical consequences have been divested of their former subtleties and are made openly

8. See A. S. Miller, "A Note on the Criticism of Supreme Court Decisions," 10 *Journal of Public Law* 139 (1961).

9. See Mayo and Jones, "Legal Policy Decision Process: Alternative Thinking and the Predictive Function," 33 *George Washington Law Review* 318 (1964).

and explicitly. The Justices' reliance on practical results, however, is not yet unanimously accepted by their judicial colleagues or by the public.

The Harmonizing Function of the Supreme Court. One part of the Supreme Court's responsibilities lies in promoting harmony and unity among the lower courts. This it does by resolving inconsistencies of constitutional or statutory interpretation, by promoting adherence to precedent, and, at least nominally, by formulating and thereafter supervising observance below of the federal rules of procedure. This function emphasizes the apparent unity of the three levels of the national judicial system and helps give it a misleadingly monolithic appearance.

Another factor that seemingly joins the Supreme Court to the lower tribunals in a hierarchical relationship is the High Court's reputation for protecting individuals by correcting miscarriages of justice and by serving as our main line of resistance in the defense of individual rights. The Court's image as a rectifier of lower-court mistakes receives reinforcement with each decision benefiting an individual private litigant, even though the real mission of the tribunal is to prescribe or to refine general principles of public law.

The Divisive Effects of Supreme Court Activity. The High Court serves multiple ends in the constitutional scheme of things. In addition to superintending the lower courts, it functions as arbiter of federal-state relations according to its prevailing view of constitutional principles. It also helps preserve the balance of constitutional power between the three branches of government, protects constitutionally guaranteed rights and liberties, and maintains the effectiveness of governmental power.

Though the lower courts are also obligated to serve many of these same enduring general needs of the constitutional system, the High Court may still be drawn into conflict with particular lower courts. Since the High Court's purposes and outlook are different from those of inferior national courts, its conclusions —drawn from different premises or reached by different courses of public policy development—may readily clash with theirs. The Justices on such occasions are free, and may feel compelled, to substitute their views of substantive principle for those of the lower courts. In doing so, they can disregard parochial considerations of local preference and substitute whatever they regard to be more imperatively required by broader issues of constitutional principle or national policy. No matter what may have been the origin or nature of the cases enabling it to do so, fulfillment by the High Court of its various substantive roles may pull it away from the inferior courts. Thus the lower courts are set apart as one identifiable segment of the system and the Supreme Court as the other and more authoritative portion.

RELATIONS BETWEEN THE LEVELS

The suggestion that the pyramidal arrangement of national courts brings with it all of the usual characteristics of hierarchical control is severely misleading. It is easy to exaggerate the ability of the High Court as "hierarchical superior" to control the inferior levels, but in fact the inferior courts are created by statute as semiautonomous units of judicial administration having their own organic position, jurisdiction, and identity independent of the will of the Supreme Court. Unlike most hierarchical structures, the constitutional courts lack the usual formal superior-subordinate relationships.

For one thing, higher-court judges have nothing to do with hiring the subordinate judges. Since superior judges do not delegate authority to inferior judges, they cannot recall that authority should it be misused. Like other mortals, judges may be subject to the weaknesses of human nature. Some have been lethargic or indifferent; some have remained on their benches too long and become senile; some have been excessive drinkers; and some have been rendered incapable of performing their duties by unacknowledged illness. A few have yielded to venality and dispensed justice for personal gain. But not even the Supreme Court can dismiss an inferior-court judge, however insubordinate, slothful, senile, disrespectful, or unheeding of higher-court precedents he may be.

Another point is that clear two-way open lines of communication between the levels and units of the judiciary are, unlike those of a normal scalar arrangement, virtually nonexistent. The High Court is not consulted by the inferior courts on matters of policy growing out of the decision of individual cases, and a subordinate judge does not submit his decisions and opinions to higher authority before making them public.

Moreover, even the effectiveness of the appeals mechanism

as a means of controlling lower courts is limited. First of all, federal lower-court judges are subject to direction, supervision, or control by judicial superiors only to the degree that litigants make appeals. Though each lower-court judge works subject to the *possibility* of review above, he knows that initiative for review does not rest with the higher court.

Also, with regard to the Supreme Court, it *can* review lower-court decisions, but the chances of its doing so are exceedingly slim. The odds are so great against a lower court's being subjected to close supervision in this way that operational control by the High Court over the lower tribunals is more presumed than real.

Should the case reach the highest level, in formal terms, of course, a Supreme Court decision is binding on the lower federal courts, and all the judges of those tribunals are supposedly obligated to observe it. But there is apt to be a gap between actual practice and the approved pattern of the working relationship. Impact studies show that lower-court judges do not always faithfully follow the decisions of higher authority.[10] Although lower-court judges are for the most part acutely conscious of their obligations and in fact do fulfill them, some decisions of the Supreme Court have seemed so unpalatable to certain inferior-court judges as to be impossible for them to swallow. There are few, if any, instances when the Supreme Court can make its will effectively binding on the lower tribunals if the lower courts are not disposed to cooperate by following the High Court's lead. Thus, even the appellate step does not always give the Supreme Court the last word.

Despite all this, there is an unspoken assumption that the inferior judges will follow precedent, respect the authority of higher tribunals in implementing their orders, and observe the formal rules of the United States courts. Formal deference and respect do characterize the usual pattern of relations between the judges of superior and subordinate tribunals. Appellate-court judge Calvin Magruder has revealed his sense of the amenities that his position imposed upon him in his relations

10. For example, see S. L. Wasby, *The Impact of the United States Supreme Court: Some Perspectives* (Dorsey Press, 1970), and T. L. Becker, *The Impact of Supreme Court Decisions* (Oxford University Press, 1969). Both books provide references to additional studies, usually of a specific nature.

with federal trial judges.[11] Such judicial etiquette is observed also in dealings with the Supreme Court, and it emerges mainly from the institutional prestige accorded to the various courts.

From the above we might conclude that the federal court system is probably too loosely structured to be called "integrated." "Articulated" may be a better word to describe the way in which its parts work together.

11. "The Trials and Tribulations of an Intermediate Appellate Court," 44 *Cornell Law Quarterly* 1 (1958).

CHAPTER 2

The Formal Structure of the Courts: Organization and Jurisdiction

This chapter will serve as a refresher for those who already have a clear understanding of the structure and competences of the various constitutional courts of the national judiciary, and it will provide necessary background for those who have not already gained it from other sources.

However sterile this material may seem, its importance cannot be gainsaid. For it is the jurisdictional delineation that determines what a court can do—what issues it can address, what processes it can employ, what qualifications its judges must have, who can have access to it, for what purposes its authority can be invoked, and a host of similar aspects of its operation that collectively define it as a court. Hence, such considerations should be taken to heart, for they provide the framework within which the political and human forces operate. It is the political and human forces that we will focus on in the remainder of this book.

THE REGULAR CONSTITUTIONAL COURTS

The "regular" constitutional courts of the United States are what most people have in mind when they think of justice being administered by "federal courts," or of a defendant as being tried by a "national court," federal and national being used synonymously. These courts are created pursuant to the declaration of Article III of the Constitution that "the judicial power of the United States shall be vested in one Supreme Court and in such inferior courts as the Congress may from time to time ordain and establish." Article III courts exercise only "judicial power" of the United States in the settlement of cases and controversies, but they can be required by statutes enacted under Congress' enumerated powers to perform other functions such as administration of rules and regulations for the control of bankruptcies, or for granting citizenship by means of naturalization. They are usually thought of as a three-layered hierarchy of tribunals, with a broad base of trial courts, a much narrower center layer of appellate courts, and a peak comprised of one Supreme Court of the United States to which all "inferior"[1] courts and their judges are subordinated and by which they are effectively controlled. However, a major purpose of the examination that follows will be to explore the realities of this conception and to see to what extent the theoretical characteristics of a "hierarchical system" are present in actual intercourt relations.

Although "regular" courts have varied in number and kind from period to period since 1789,[2] the "inferior" tribunals are now of two types: the United States District Courts and, above them, the United States Courts of Appeals. In all of their aspects these are wholly the creation of Congress, although in assigning them competence to decide cases and controversies arising under the Constitution, laws, and treaties of the United States, the discretion of Congress is confined to those categories of jurisdiction enumerated by Article III of the Constitution. Hence, "regular" constitutional courts exercise only the judicial power of the United States, and they may only *decide* those cases and controversies which arise under the Constitution, laws,

1. "Inferior" is the constitutional term designating Article III tribunals created by Congress below the Supreme Court. It suggests that such courts are judicially subordinate or junior in authority to the Supreme Court, but it in no way connotes that these courts or their personnel are morally inferior or of lesser quality or entitled to lesser respect as agents of judicial power.

2. An interesting discussion of the historic evolution of the national court system can be found in Robert J. McCloskey, *The American Supreme Court* (University of Chicago Press, 1960), ch. 2, and in R. J. Richardson and K. Vines, *The Politics of Federal Courts* (Little, Brown, 1970), ch. 2.

and treaties of the United States. Moreover, the Constitution provides that their judges are protected by the guarantees of an irreducible salary during continuance in office and of tenure during "good behavior." Because they can only exercise judicial power to decide cases and controversies, they may not give "advisory opinions" on legal questions, even ones arising under the Constitution, statutes made in pursuance of it, or treaties made under authority of the United States.

ORGANIZATION OF THE REGULAR CONSTITUTIONAL COURTS

The United States District Courts. District Courts of the United States are the trial courts of the federal judicial system and possess only original jurisdiction. In fiscal 1972 they numbered 90 and had authorized for them 400 active and 92 senior judges, many of whom carried substantial caseloads.[3] Each tribunal presides over a jurisdictional area known as a "district" which consists of an entire state or a portion thereof, but court is held within the states at approximately 350 different places of venue as designated by law. No district embraces more than one state and none cuts across state boundaries to include parts of two or more states. At mid-1973, twenty-six states and the District of Columbia each comprised a district containing one District Court; twelve states were divided so each contained two District Courts; nine so as each contained three; and Texas, California, and New York each contained four.

The Use of Juries. Among the regular constitutional courts of the United States only the District Courts use juries. The right to trial by jury in national courts is constitutionally guaranteed in civil and criminal trials. It may be waived in both, however, by the defendant with permission of the court and prosecution, and in civil trials it is guaranteed only if the amount in controversy is more than twenty dollars.

The use of juries is probably less common than myths sup-

---

3. *Annual Report of the Director, Administrative Office of the United States Courts* (Government Printing Office, 1973), p. 90. This volume contains comprehensive statistical data on the work of the regular constitutional courts. Hereafter cited as *Annual Report of the Director,* 1973.

The above figures include the District of Columbia, but not Puerto Rico, Virgin Islands, Canal Zone, or Guam.

porting the virtues of trial by jury may lead general opinion to believe. During the twelve-month period ending June 30, 1973, 8,297 civil suits were completed by trial. Of that number, juries were employed in only 3,380 cases—less than half of the total.[4] During that same period, 8,571 criminal trials were completed, of which 5,644 employed juries.[5] Hence, 65 percent of the criminal defendants opted for juries. It may seem from these figures that defense attorneys calculate their clients to have a better chance to be found not guilty if a jury hears the evidence, but the fact is that judges acquitted 29 percent (or 690) of the defendants tried without juries, whereas juries acquitted only 27 percent (or 1,387) of those tried before their peers.[6]

Although federal criminal-trial juries continue to employ the traditional twelve members, 59 of the 94 District Courts by local rule have adopted the reduced jury of six persons for civil trials. Others by agreement of counsel permit fewer than twelve jurors. The smaller size has expedited completion of the jury selection process and enabled courts to move cases more rapidly toward final disposition.

District-Court Workload. It is before the District Courts that constitutionally prescribed procedural guarantees have their most frequent application and greatest value, for it is in these courts that most civil and criminal cases arising under national law originate and terminate. Hence, it is here that the protections of due process of law, immunity from compulsory self-incrimination and unreasonable searches and seizures, indictment by grand jury and trial by petit jury, the right of confrontation, and the other guarantees found principally in the Bill of Rights have optimum value.

As the principal workhorses of the national court system, the District Courts are mainly concerned with the handling of civil and criminal cases. During the fiscal year ending June 30, 1973, they received by filing 98,560 civil and 42,434 criminal cases

4. A trial, as that term is used here, refers to a contested proceeding (other than a hearing on a motion) before either a jury or court in which evidence was introduced and a final judgment was sought. *Annual Report of the Director*, 1973, table C–4, p. 358.

5. Ibid., table C–7, p. 378.

6. Ibid.

and terminated 98,259 civil and 43,456 criminal cases.[7] But during the same period they also received 104,213 petitions for naturalization and naturalized 98,555 aliens, processed 139,356 passport applications,[8] and began 173,197 and terminated 180,467 proceedings in bankruptcy.[9] In addition, the District Courts carried on other categories of business of lesser note but requiring the attention of their judges. Some indication of the growth of workload carried by these courts and of the current status of combined civil and criminal dockets can be obtained from Table 1.

The caseload per judge varies greatly from one district to another,[10] and although the situation is improving under the watchful eyes of the Administrative Office of United States Courts, the lower-court conferences and councils, and the Judicial Conference of the United States, noticeable differences in levels of judicial output can be found among the district judges. Some dockets are heavy,[11] and judges keep pace, if indeed they are able to do so, only by exerting maximum effort; at the same time, the eased condition of dockets in other, less busy, districts permits their judges to accept temporary assignments in districts where the caseload has become excessive. In 1973, for all District Courts, an average of 367 cases were filed,

7. For civil and criminal case data see *Annual Report of the Director*, 1973, table 13, p. 115.
Cases may be "terminated" or "disposed of" by trial. Both terms are used in civil proceedings to mean that the cases have been withdrawn, defaulted, compromised before or during trial, or in some other way brought to a conclusion; and in criminal prosecutions to mean that the cases have been disposed of by guilty pleas with or without plea bargaining, by being nolle prossed, by being dismissed for lack of evidence, or by additional methods other than verdict following trial.
8. *Annual Report of the Director*, 1973, table P–1, p. 482.
9. Ibid., table F–1, p. 449.
10. Since 1962 the federal courts have been using a weighted filings index for making comparisons of the workloads of courts with widely divergent caseload mixes. Classes of cases are weighted according to the expected amount of court time required for disposition. The weighting system is explained in the *Annual Report of the Director*, 1971, pp. 167–183. Weightings for the period ending June 30, 1973, can be found in ibid., 1973, pp. 216–218 and in table X–1a, pp. 502–505, and table X–1b, pp. 506–508.
11. In 1972, 50 percent of all dispositions by all District Courts were made by those in the twelve major metropolitan centers of the nation.

TABLE 1

U.S. DISTRICT COURTS,
TOTAL CIVIL AND CRIMINAL CASES,
1940, 1950, 1960, 1969–1973

Fiscal Year	Authorized Judgeships, as of June 30	Filed	Terminated	Pending on June 30
1940	183	68,235	71,228	39,031
1950	218	92,342	90,673	63,784
1960	245	89,112	91,693	68,942
1969	341	112,606	105,760	104,091
1970	401	127,280	117,254	114,117
1971	401	136,553	126,145	124,525
1972	400	145,227	143,282	126,470
1973	400	140,994	141,715	125,749
Percent change in 1973 over:				
1940	118.6	106.6	98.9	222.2
1960	63.3	58.2	54.5	82.4
1972	0.0	—2.9	1.1	—0.6

SOURCE: *Annual Report of the Director*, 1973, Table 13, p. 115.

369 were terminated, and 327 were left pending for each district judge in regular service.

The problem of heavy docket-loads is reflected in the length of time cases await final disposition. Of civil cases pending on June 30, 1973, 59,957 had been waiting less than one year, 23,036 had been pending from one to two years, 9,842 from two to three years, and 7,602 for three years or more.[12] Concentrated effort is made to move criminal cases forward as expeditiously as considerations of fairness and other conditions permit, especially if the defendant is in custody awaiting trial. There is less urgency if the defendant is awaiting trial "on the street," but even then undue delay is undesirable. When the defendant is a fugitive, trial is delayed until he is apprehended. This fact in large measure accounts for the large number of long-pending cases, as shown in Table 2.

12. *Annual Report of the Director*, 1973, table C–6a, p. 372.

TABLE 2

U.S. DISTRICT COURTS,
CRIMINAL CASES PENDING JUNE 30, 1973

	Pending less than 6 mos.	Pending without fugitive defendants	Pending with fugitive defendants
Pending 6 to 12 mos.		2,343	1,025
Pending 1 to 2 yrs.		2,418	3,410
Pending 3 or more yrs.		353	2,883
Subtotals	11,804	5,114	7,498
Aggregate total	24,416		

SOURCE: *Annual Report of the Director*, 1973, Table D–8b, p. 436.

To reduce the pendency of criminal cases, Rule 50(b), Federal Rules of Criminal Procedure, was adopted effective October 1, 1972. It provides that each District Court shall have a plan for the prompt disposition of criminal cases, including rules fixing time limits within which procedures before and during trial and sentencing must take place. Under it, each court is to have a means for reporting the status of cases and other matters. Rule 50(b) also requires each District Court to carry on continuous study of its administration of criminal justice.

Every court has established a pattern of time limits in response to Rule 50(b), but much variation exists in the periods adopted. For example, the range of limits within which arraignment of a defendant in custody must take place extends from seven days in Alaska to sixty days in the Middle District of Georgia. The most commonly used limit is the twenty or twenty-five days adopted by fifty District Courts. Time limits for the trial of defendants in custody range from a low of forty-five days in three districts up to 120 days in one. Seventy-five District Courts have adopted a limit of ninety days.

Time limits from conviction to sentencing also vary widely among the districts. Four have fixed fifteen-day limits, one a sixty-five day period, and fifty-eight Districts use a maximum of forty-five days. In every instance, however, the time limits set for defendants not in custody are more lenient than the ones mentioned above.[13]

Rule 50(b) has not been long in operation. But it probably deserves some credit for the fact that in fiscal 1973 terminations of criminal cases exceeded filings by 1,022 and reduced the number of pending criminal cases for the first time since 1969.

A crowded docket, of course, can be cleared by Congress' adding to the number of judges permanently assigned to a court or by the Chief Justice of the United States, who can provide for temporary and usually brief transfers of "visiting" judges from their own to other and more congested courts.

Every District Court has permanently assigned to it at least one judge, and the largest District Court has twenty-seven judges. The number assigned bears a reasonable but not care-fully measured relationship to the volume of business handled by each court.[14] Each one-judge tribunal or division of a multiple-judge court is ordinarily presided over by a single judge. Not even the use of one-judge panels by multiple-judge courts, however, is necessarily adequate to keep their calendars clear.

Occasionally, creation by Congress of an additional district tribunal will relieve the pressure of litigation in a given state, but such *ad hoc* responses to the problem of court workload have thus far proven to be of only limited avail. As Henry J. Abraham has said, there is "perpetually an insufficient number" of district judges.[15] In recent decades the number seems to have

13. *Annual Report of the Director*, 1973, Appendix IV, table 1, pp. 769–774. Only the shortest, longest, and most widely used limits for each phase of the criminal justice process have been identified here. Hence, the numbers of District Courts counted will not add up to the number of existing courts.

14. During the fiscal year ending June 30, 1973, the 25 largest District Courts (having 58.3 percent of the authorized judgeships) terminated 59.4 percent of civil cases (58,391) terminated by all District Courts, received 57.3 percent of those commenced in all District Courts, and had pending as of the close of the year 60.3 percent (61,125) of the whole number of civil cases remaining. For the prior one-year period, the data were: terminated, 60.4 percent (57,451); commenced, 58.3 percent (56,030); pending, 62.4 percent (63,072). Data adapted from *Annual Report of the Director*, 1973, table 31, p. 149.

15. *The Judicial Process*, 3rd ed. (Oxford University Press, 1975), p. 158.

been regularly inadequate for the process of adjudication to keep pace with the growth of the nation and the litigation that conflict in society produces.

The pressure of new suits on the courts, the poor production records of some individual judges, and a shortage of jurists only partly account for the backlog of cases. Other factors also contribute to the slow pace of adjudication and to the failure of District Courts to keep their dockets current. Part of the problem of case backlog arises from the sometime lethargy, procrastination, or other unhappy traits of judges. Aside from the fact that some civil and criminal trials are very protracted and retard the trial court's ability to cope with its caseload, deliberate stalling tactics by counsel are common and add immeasurably to the time required to dispose of suits. Too lenient granting of delays by a judge, baseless requests for continuances, deliberate failure by counsel to prepare for trial and their refusal to cooperate in pre-trial or other informal means of disposition, failure of witnesses to appear, raising of collateral issues that necessitate hearings and permit appeals, as well as a host of other features of court procedure make it difficult for the most ambitious and conscientious jurist to keep his calendar up to date.

Criminal Jurisdiction. The jurisdiction of the District Courts embraces a wide variety of acts that federal statutes define as criminal. A table of cases by category of major crimes prosecuted in these tribunals embraces about fifty classifications, of which a representative sample includes interstate transportation of stolen property; breaking and entering; embezzlement; fraud; engaging in "white slavery"; offenses under the narcotics, food, drug, cosmetic, and antitrust statutes; impersonation; treason; espionage; sedition; sabotage; counterfeiting; prison escape; rioting; offenses against copyright, customs, patent, and postal regulations; kidnaping; violations of firearms, internal revenue, and national primary and election laws and laws regulating campaign and party finances; and many others.

Congress has utilized its authority over commerce to make certain activities criminal. Thus it is a federal crime to transport across state lines stolen property, switchblade knives, slot machines, kidnaped persons, fugitives, or women for immoral purposes; also mislabeled foods, drugs, and cosmetics or ones containing harmful ingredients. Authority to make other activities come under national law derives from congressional power to provide for a system of coinage and currency. Thus debasement of specie and other acts that would threaten the integrity of the monetary system are federal crimes. Another category of federal jurisdiction comes from congressional power to establish and operate a postal system. Still another comes from its power to provide for the existence and maintenance of military forces and to protect the national security by providing for the punishment of actions apt to imperil or weaken the national posture.

Further authority to define crimes against United States statutes arises from the place at which the act was committed. Congress' power to control activities on federal lands and in federal buildings and other property enables it to proscribe certain actions by declaring them to be criminal. To rob a bank chartered by Congress is a national offense; to burgle the shoe store next door to it is not, unless it is on a military post or is in some other manner brought under federal jurisdiction.

Whatever the specific nature of the crime, its criminality must be traceable to a statute, for there are no federal common-law crimes. All federal crimes are defined by enacted statute or by constitutional provision, and the failure of Congress to assign responsibility for their enforcement to the courts of the several states is a matter of policy rather than of constitutional necessity. The Constitutional Convention might have chosen to have national prosecutors take criminal cases under national law into the courts of the several states. (Indeed, Congress has occasionally used this arrangement: for example, to try prosecutions growing out of the Fugitive Slave Laws and the Emergency Price Control Act.) But the Convention chose instead to authorize Congress to create a system of national courts and to vest criminal jurisdiction in them. The resulting criminal litigation has reached considerable proportions, as can be seen in Table 3. Nevertheless, in spite of the broad scope of the District Courts' criminal jurisdiction and the long catalog of national crimes, most crimes in the United States are prosecuted under state law before state tribunals.

Civil Jurisdiction. No objection seems to exist in principle against leaving to state tribunals enforcement of all or most civil wrongs for which remedies are provided by national law. To do so is, in fact, part of their obligation within the federal scheme under the Constitution, except as exclusive jurisdiction has been placed by statute in the District Courts. Congress, in

TABLE 3

U.S. DISTRICT COURTS,
TOTAL CRIMINAL CASES,
1940, 1950, 1960, 1969–1973

Fiscal Year	Authorized Judgeships, as of June 30	Filed	Terminated	Pending on June 30
1940	183	33,401	33,861	9,553
1950	218	37,720	37,414	8,181
1960	245	29,828	29,864	7,691
1969	341	35,413	32,406	17,770
1970	401	39,959	36,819	20,910
1971	401	43,157	39,582	24,485
1972	400	49,054	48,101	25,438
1973	400	42,434	43,456	24,416
Percent change in 1973 over:				
1940	118.6	27.0	28.3	155.6
1960	63.3	42.2	45.5	217.5
1972	0.0	−13.5	−9.7	−4.0

SOURCE: *Annual Report of the Director*, 1973, Table 13, p. 115.

fact, has been sparing in assigning exclusive jurisdiction to the District Courts and has limited it to certain categories of civil actions, such as those arising under bankruptcy acts, admiralty and maritime law, and patent and copyright statutes. Nevertheless, some practical advantages grow out of recognizing that, in general, federal law should be enforced by federal judges in federal courts. Only thereby can greater expertise be cultivated, can greater uniformity be injected into the whole body of federal law, and can the need for Supreme Court review be significantly diminished. But for the federal trial courts to try every civil action arising under the constitutionally permissible scope of civil jurisdiction in a nation of 220 million people would require a tremendous expansion in the number of trial judges.

The workload of civil cases has also grown steadily, as the data in Table 4 reveal.

TABLE 4

U.S. DISTRICT COURTS,
TOTAL CIVIL CASES,
1940, 1950, 1960, 1969–1973

Fiscal Year	Authorized Judgeships, as of June 30	Filed	Terminated	Pending on June 30
1940	183	34,734	37,367	29,478
1950	218	54,622	53,259	55,603
1960	245	59,284	61,829	61,251
1969	341	77,193	73,354	86,321
1970	401	87,321	80,435	93,207
1971	401	93,396	86,563	100,040
1972	400	96,173	95,181	101,032
1973	400	98,560	98,259	101,333
Percent change in 1973 over:				
1940	118.6	183.8	163.0	243.8
1960	63.3	66.3	58.9	65.4
1972	0.0	2.5	3.2	0.3

SOURCE: *Annual Report of the Director*, 1973, Table 13, p. 115.

More than one-quarter, or 25,415, of the 98,259 civil cases terminated during the fiscal year ending June 30, 1973, were "diversity" cases.[16] The jurisdiction of these cases grows out of the "diversity clause" of Article III, which permits a citizen of one state to bring a civil action in the appropriate District Court of the United States against a citizen of a second state.

16. Court action was required for 15,047 diversity dispositions, of which 4,785 came before trial, 6,636 during or after pretrial, and 3,626 during or after trial. The total of diversity cases reaching trial was 14.3 percent. See *Annual Report of the Director*, 1973, table C–4, p. 359. Additional diversity cases almost equal in number (25,281) to those terminated were commenced during fiscal 1973. These included 10,543 disputes over contracts, 58 stockholders' suits, 745 suits over real property, and 13,167 suits for damages growing out of personal injuries (divided almost equally between automobile-accident injury and "other personal injury"). Ibid., table X–2, pp. 510–511.

Diversity suits were made federal in character only to assure than neither party would gain advantage over the other in a tribunal of one party's state. They are purely private actions arising out of disputes involving state laws, and they often require federal district judges to apply state law to their resolution. Diversity suits are often long and complex, and their great number requires much time and energy of the District Courts.

To curtail the number of diversity cases eligible for trial by District Courts, Congress has declared by statute that the amount in controversy must be $10,000 or more. Even then, the action *may* be heard in a state court, and if the amount in dispute is less than $10,000 it must be heard in a state court. For purposes of diversity jurisdiction, a corporation is accepted as being a "citizen," whether it be plaintiff or defendant, and this fact greatly increases the number of such suits brought to the District Courts.

Diversity cases make up what is probably the most unjustifiable category of civil actions triable in United States District Courts. Their disposition by a national constitutional court rarely affords any advantage to the general well-being of the people, to the national government, or to the judiciary, and a demand has arisen that national jurisdiction over them be curtailed or abolished. Critics of the constitutional diversity jurisdiction insist that whatever justification for it may have existed at one time, its validity today is at best controversial. They believe that there is no longer any need for such a safeguard against unfair, biased, or discriminatory administration of justice by a state court in a civil action when the defendant is a citizen of a different state. The critics also argue that elimination of this class of actions from federal jurisdiction would go far toward enabling the existing number of judges to handle the burden of their remaining civil business. In particular, they believe such a measure would enable judges to get at those civil actions that under existing conditions are too often pushed aside because they threaten to be long, complex, and technical. Also, a greater number of simple actions could be disposed of and the dockets be kept reasonably current.

Although diversity actions comprise a significant part of the civil cases brought to District Courts, statutory sources of jurisdiction of course provide a substantial part of District Court litigation. During the fiscal year ending June 30, 1973, the United States was plaintiff in 13,881 civil suits brought under labor, tax, antitrust, and an unspecified miscellany of other statutes. It was defendant in 13,606 suits brought under such acts as the Federal Tort Claims Act, Social Security Act, and the internal revenue laws. Federal questions were raised in 43,291 actions involving marine contracts, the Jones Merchant Seamen's Act, the Federal Employer's Liability Act, labor cases, petitions for writs of habeas corpus, antitrust acts, copyrights and trademarks, civil rights, and patents.[17]

Civil suits have been the basis for many District Court decisions raising important questions of governmental policy and of constitutional law. Such actions have ultimately settled the authority of Congress to regulate the intrastate rates of railroads so that localities and persons would be protected from discriminatory treatment. Such decisions have sustained the power of Congress to utilize the Interstate Commerce Commission to recover income of railroads earned above a fair return; thus the recaptured earnings could be used to build up a system of national railroads sufficient to handle all the interstate traffic of the country, and yet the carriers would be able to earn enough to maintain safety and efficiency in their operations. District Court decisions have upheld the powers of the Federal Communications Commission to renew or refuse to renew the licenses of radio broadcasting stations. In a long series of actions brought under the antitrust laws, the District Courts have upheld the power of Congress to restrain trusts and monopoly agreements, thus establishing and maintaining a policy of free competition. And they have sustained application of the antitrust laws to local labor activities that impede the movement of goods in interstate commerce.

And yet, although the facts of any civil or criminal case have a potential for generating a precedent-setting decision, the truth remains that proportional to the total number of dispositions made, important implications for public policy infrequently emerge from District Court decisions. District Courts are more important in the judicial system as mechanisms for applying and enforcing policies identified and enunciated from above. Major Supreme Court decisions often generate litigation for resolution by trial and intermediate appellate courts. A precedent-setting Supreme Court decision can be counted upon to stimulate a wave of litigation based upon the newly enunciated principle.

17. Ibid., table X–2, pp. 510–511.

Each successive surge of cases enables the lower courts to define and refine the new area of doctrine in process; when the law becomes sufficiently clarified for practical application, the influx of cases subsides. The national trial courts are also important as sources of disputed interpretations of national statutes from which precedent-setting decisions by higher courts can arise.

Unlike the federal District Courts, federal appellate courts are presented with fewer matters of enforcement and with more numerous questions of policy. As a rough rule of thumb, it seems safe to say that a larger percent of broad policy questions will be decided by the higher courts than by lower ones. Whenever a novel constitutional challenge is made or a broad policy issue of general law is raised, the District Court decision is almost certain to be appealed because of its implications for interests beyond those of the immediate parties.

Three-Judge District Courts. A third type of Article III lower tribunal has been brought into being by congressional act. Specific courts are created *ad hoc* as needed, the panels disbanding when the judicial business that called each into being has been disposed of. Their judges are drawn from the benches of district and intermediate courts, and each court consists of three members instead of the single judge who normally presides over a trial court. The use of these courts is mandatory for limited categories of litigation that various statutes have directed shall be tried by a special three-judge District Court. Hence, these tribunals are hybrids—they are Article III courts, but they are so obviously "special purpose" courts that they are more like such units as the Court of Claims than regular District Courts.

Because these special courts provide a mode of judicial relief different from the ordinary constitutional courts through which "federal" questions normally move, Congress by a series of statutes has mandated their use for the resolution of a small number of questions important either to individual rights, to governmental processes, or to the general welfare. Three-judge courts may be convened by the Chief Judge of the Circuit whenever a litigant in a regular District Court seeks to enjoin, on the grounds of its alleged unconstitutionality, an order of the Interstate Commerce Commission; or the enforcement, operation, or execution of an act of Congress, a state statute, or an administrative order of a state agency. In addition, certain suits arising under antitrust laws, reapportionment issues, civil rights acts (including the 1965 Voting Rights Act), and the internal revenue code must be handled by one of these special courts. Because of the unusual significance of the specified issues or the potential far-reaching consequences of stopping by injunction the wheels of national or state statutory implementation, three judicial minds instead of one make an initial resolution. Each panel must include at least one appellate judge and one district judge, but normally two district judges and one appellate judge sit on a court. The final point to be noted is that Congress, to expedite resolution of the important issues it has entrusted to three-judge courts for resolution, has provided that appeal from their decision shall lie as a matter of right directly to the Supreme Court, bypassing the Courts of Appeals.

During the fiscal year ending June 30, 1973, 474 requests for three-judge courts went before the District Courts, but only 320 were empaneled to hold hearings. Reviews of Interstate Commerce Commission orders accounted for 52, civil rights cases for 166, reapportionment suits for 7, and hearings on state or local regulations for 79. Their rate of use has increased dramatically from 1969, when only three were requested and one held. It should be remembered that such courts are composed of judges who must set aside their regular work to serve on them.

In sum, these courts are distinguished by the number of their judges, their *ad hoc* composition, their lack of general jurisdiction, and their identification with the circuit within which the controversy arose. Although they are not parts of the regular system of constitutional tribunals, they are so closely entwined with it that they are given this brief notice. The original reason for their creation was to curb the power of a single judge to enjoin enforcement of an act of a state legislature; later, their use was broadened to protect acts of Congress from the idiosyncrasies of a single judge.

Whatever the justifications advanced originally for them, their continuation has come under attack. They provide an important additional mode of judicial conflict-resolution and of speedy and direct access to the Supreme Court, but their use disrupts the conduct of judicial business in the courts whose judges are called away, bypasses the Courts of Appeals, and produces only a trial-court record unrefined by appellate-level research, briefs, arguments, and analysis which may later aid the Supreme Court. Moreover, the Justices reportedly feel that it is mandatory that they undertake serious review of appeals from three-judge decisions, for otherwise the appellant would be deprived of all review. The Chief Justice, Warren Burger, would like therefore to dispense with three-judge District Courts.[18]

The United States Courts of Appeals.   Next above the District Courts are the ten regular Courts of Appeals, one for each of the circuits into which the United States is divided, and an eleventh created for the District of Columbia. Each circuit consists of several states, ranging from three (Second Circuit: New York, Vermont, and Connecticut) to nine (Ninth Circuit: Alaska, Arizona, California, Hawaii, Idaho, Montana, Nevada, Oregon, Washington, and the district of Guam). These courts review the decisions of District Courts located within their circuits. Thus the litigation heard by the Courts of Appeals falls into much the same classes as do the cases tried by the District Courts. And because it is so difficult to take cases to the Supreme Court, the Courts of Appeals represent the end of the line for many litigants.

The caseloads of the appellate courts have grown steadily for the last seventeen years. During the fiscal year ending June 30, 1973, the caseload reached an all-time high, with 15,629 cases filed, 15,112 disposed of, and 10,456 remaining pending.[19]

Most of their appellate business comes from the District Courts. More than thirteen thousand (13,329) appeals were taken to the appellate courts from the district tribunals, but only 1,616 came from boards and commissions.[20] Civil actions accounted for 8,876 appeals, and 4,453 were appeals in criminal cases.[21] Hence, approximately 10 percent of the cases terminated

18. See speech before the American Bar Association, San Francisco, 14 August 1972, "Report on Problems of the Judiciary." Interview, *U.S. News and World Report*, 21 August 1972, p. 41.

19. *Annual Report of the Director*, 1973, p. 95.

20. *Annual Report of the Director*, 1973, table 5, p. 104. Appeals from administrative boards and commissions originated as follows: Tax Court, 241; Civil Aeronautics Board, 58; Federal Communications Commission, 75; Federal Power Commission, 128; Federal Trade Commission, 23; National Labor Relations Board, 612; Securities and Exchange Commission, 20; Secretary of Agriculture, 5; Immigration and Naturalization Service, 228; all other boards and commissions, 226. Ibid., table B–3, p. 306.

21. Ibid., table 5, p. 105.

by District Courts were taken to the Courts of Appeals between July 1, 1972 and June 30, 1973.

Reversal rates by Courts of Appeals of cases disposed of after hearing or submission was 17.5 percent. Most reversals were of civil and bankruptcy cases; only 374 criminal decisions were overturned. In summary form, these data are presented in Table 5. The appeals from the trial courts came as matters of appellants' right and could not be rejected, whatever the reviewing court may have thought about the merits of arguments advanced for taking the case upward.

TABLE 5

U.S. COURTS OF APPEALS,
REVERSAL RATE OF CASES TERMINATED
AFTER ORAL HEARING OR SUBMISSION,
FISCAL YEAR ENDED JUNE 30, 1973

Type of Case	Terminations	Reversed or Denied	Percent Reversed or Denied
Civil	5,686	1,144	20.1
Criminal	2,995	374	12.5
Bankruptcy	188	47	25.0
Administrative	725	115	15.9
Totals	9,594	1,680	17.9

SOURCE: *Annual Report of the Directors*, 1973, Table 4, p. 102.

In earlier times, Justices of the Supreme Court were obliged to "ride circuit" and sit as trial judges. The famous opinion in *Ex parte Merryman*[22] was written by "Taney, Circuit Justice" although he was Chief Justice of the United States at the time. But in time, the ages of the Justices, bad travel conditions, the press of Supreme Court business, lack of time, summer heat, and the dissipation of energy involved caused the practice to stop long before it was formally abolished. Today, the Justices are still formally "assigned" to the several circuits and on very

22. Fed. Case No. 9487 (1861).

rare occasions sit in an appellate court. Beyond that, however, their main responsibility in connection with their circuit assignment is to participate in meetings of the Judicial Conferences of their respective Circuits and to provide contact and liaison between the courts of the Circuits and the Supreme Court.

The authorized total number of judges on the Courts of Appeals is 97. The number of regularly assigned judges on each of the eleven Courts varies considerably: currently from three in the First Circuit to fifteen in the Fifth. After a judge has been appointed he must reside in the circuit to which he is assigned. Although the full bench may meet *en banc* to hear and decide an especially important or troublesome case, only three judges, of whom two constitute a quorum for decision, need hear every case. Meetings in regular term are held at statutorily designated cities located within the respective circuits (e.g., the Fourth Circuit Court of Appeals regularly convenes at Richmond, Virginia, and at Winston Salem, North Carolina), but any court may meet for extraordinary reasons in special term at any place within its circuit. Only when a court of more than three judges convenes to hear a case *en banc* do all members of a Court of Appeals assemble at the place of meeting. When, as is the usual practice, it operates through panels of three judges, it is necessary only for the panels to assemble at their respective geographically separated sites within the circuit.

To prevent the formation of permanent panels of like-thinking judges, the Chief Judge of the Court is supposed to provide for automatic rotation of judicial personnel among panels. The assignment commissioner assigns cases to the different panels in such a way that from the time an appeal is perfected until the assignment is announced the parties cannot know which judges will hear their case. However, as will be further examined below, there is reason to suspect that objective assignments are not always made.

In the course of terminating 15,112 cases during fiscal 1973 the eleven Courts of Appeals held a total of 6,555 oral hearings. Of these, only 23 cases were heard *en banc*; the other 6,532 were disposed of by three-judge panels. Twenty percent of the total were disposed of without hearings, on the record below reinforced by submitted appellate briefs.[23]

23. *Annual Report of the Director*, 1973, p. 106.

JURISDICTION OF REGULAR
CONSTITUTIONAL COURTS

The constitutional statement in Article III is one of general jurisdiction assignable at the discretion of Congress to regular federal courts.[24] That jurisdictional statement is couched in seemingly specific language but is so comprehensive as to embrace every question likely to emerge during the course of the social, political, and economic growth of the nation; and it is upon these provisions that the entire system of social control, implemented by national laws enforced by national courts, is based. Congressional authority to control jurisdiction within Article III is so definitive that even the Supreme Court is assumed not to have jurisdiction in the absence of explicit statutory grant; and that Court has not, according to Robert Stern and Joel Gressman, discovered any limitation on this Congressional authority.[25]

Courts of law can act only within the scope of their respective jurisdictions, which must be defined in reasonably precise and understandable terms. Hence, the language of the Constitution must be refined by act of Congress to specify what the regular constitutional courts may do. However, before turning to what the specific types of existing courts have been delegated to do, we will ascertain the limits within which Congress can act to fix what each *may* do.

The jurisdictional language of Article III begins by stating succinctly that "the judicial power[26] shall extend to all cases in law and equity *arising under* the Constitution, the laws of the United States, and treaties made, or which shall be made, under their authority" without regard to the subject of the dispute. Because the article confers upon the courts only authority to *decide*, its straightforward language has been formally interpreted to exclude from the application of national judicial power all items of business that do not constitute cases or controversies

24. This, of course, does not mean that Congress may withhold from the Supreme Court its constitutionally prescribed grant of original jurisdiction also set forth in Article III.

25. *Supreme Court Practice*, 4th ed. (Bureau of National Affairs, 1969), p. 23.

26. Usually thought of as the ability of a government to provide for the enforcement of its laws by means of its own system of courts and adjudication.

capable of solution through application of judicial power. This provision means that Article III courts may not give advice and are powerless to act except when a genuine adversary relationship between actual parties separated by a real conflict of interests is *brought to them* for settlement. It also means that they may not pass judgment upon a question that for any reason has become unsuited to final *decision* by the application of judicial power (such as one that has become moot, or that by its nature is merely advisory, hypothetical, friendly, academic, or political). And although private parties may avail themselves in the regular constitutional courts of the full force of the judicial power's operation, neither they nor officials of the national government may successfully evade these limitations.

However, these formal standards mean, as do so many things, essentially what the judiciary want them to mean. Like loaded shotguns behind the door, they are available for use when needed. The fact remains that federal courts do sometimes decide cases that can be described as "phony," and federal judges do give advice, some delivered orally from the bench and some conveyed in written opinions to government officials and private individuals.

The second category of jurisdiction described in this provision of the Constitution embraces "all cases of admiralty and maritime jurisdiction." At one time, this subject matter was defined neatly by British law and practice, but today in American law it brings within federal jurisdiction all matters of law growing out of circumstances arising on the high seas or on the territorial waters or navigable inland waterways of the United States.

These two categories of jurisdiction assignable to regular constitutional courts are cast solely in terms of their subject matter. In other words, if a justiciable controversy arises under maritime jurisdiction or under the Constitution or laws of the United States or the treaties made under its authority, it is within the scope of national judicial power and may be assigned by Congress to a constitutional court by statutory delegation.

The remaining categories of potential jurisdiction set out in Article III have in common not the nature of the subject matter but rather the character of the *parties* to the controversy. Thus, any litigation to which the United States is a party; between citizens of different states; between two or more states of the Union; affecting an ambassador, public minister, or consul assigned to the United States by a foreign nation; between a state and citizens of another state; between a state or its citizens and a foreign state, or its citizens or subjects; or between citizens of the same state claiming lands under grants of different states, may, if Congress opts, be brought within the jurisdiction of regular national courts.

Several clarifying points regarding these categories of possible jurisdiction should be noted.

1) The law of the Eleventh Amendment[27] to the Constitution of the United States is too complex to analyze in detail here. But a few comments may be in order about its impact upon the jurisdiction of national courts over suits against states. Private parties without the defendant state's consent may not bring suit in a national court, but the United States or another state may sue a state without its consent in a national court. State immunity from suit in federal courts has been expanded by Supreme Court interpretation to suits brought against a state by one of its citizens, by a foreign state, or by a nationally chartered corporation. A state is suable under all of these circumstances only in one of its own courts after having given its express consent in statute defining the grounds upon which it makes itself amenable to suit.

Despite the Eleventh Amendment, however, suits can be brought against state officials (including judges and governors) alleging that they are acting or have acted under a statute attacked as in violation of national law. National courts, therefore, function as important agencies for making initial determinations in proceedings brought to test the validity of state statutes. District Courts may issue injunctions against state officials in the exercise of their discretionary duties and may enjoin enforcement of a state statute before it has been found to be in conflict with national law and before it has been put into operation or interpreted by state courts.

2) The jurisdictional statements of Article III are not mutually exclusive. Extensive overlapping among them exists.

3) Article III in effect permits Congress, to the extent that it desires, to vest any or all categories of jurisdiction in whatever national tribunals it sees fit to create. Such tribunals may

---

27. "The Judicial power of the United States shall not be construed to extend to any suit in law or equity, commenced or prosecuted against one of the United States by Citizens of another State, or by Citizens or Subjects of any Foreign State."

not be given jurisdiction falling outside these categories, but these categories need not be granted to them at all or exclusively to them. In fact, nothing on the face of the provision appears to prevent Congress from abolishing the inferior national courts and vesting any or all of the Article III jurisdiction exclusively in state courts. Hence, it is readily apparent that formal relationships between the lower courts and the Supreme Court may be determined by such political or other influences as affect congressional decision-making in the matter.

4) Congress *may* vest all or any portion of Article III jurisdiction exclusively in the inferior national courts, thereby preventing the Supreme Court from sharing in its exercise to review decisions of the lower courts.

5) Congress has seen fit to create some categories of jurisdiction exclusively vested by statute in certain of the national courts. A more detailed examination will be presented below.

6) The jurisdictional provisions of the Constitution, therefore, in combination comprise only a statement of the maximum permissible jurisdiction that Congress *may*, at its discretion, assign to the regular national constitutional tribunals.

Jurisdiction of Particular Courts. To understand the jurisdiction of the regular constitutional courts in more detail it is necessary to differentiate between two terms. First, "original" jurisdiction of a court defines its competence to hear and decide a case or controversy or otherwise to dispose of it in the first instance. Second, "appellate" jurisdiction ordinarily is utilized by a higher court to review, reverse, or sustain the final actions, decisions, or rulings of a lower court. This restriction of appellate review to *final* actions, decisions, or rulings of a lower court represents congressional policy against piecemeal reviews and is intended to promote judicial efficiency and to hasten the ultimate termination of litigation.[28]

Federal appellate jurisdiction, however, is not always limited to review of cases on which final decisions have been reached or orders issued in lower courts.[29] The Supreme Court, under its plenary control of cases coming to it by certiorari from the Courts of Appeals, can take jurisdiction whatever the status

28. See 28 U.S.C. section 1291.
29. Thus *Nixon* v. *United States*, 418 U.S. 683 (1974), went to the Supreme Court on a petition for certiorari before judgment, as did President Nixon's cross-petition for certiorari before judgment in *United States* v. *Nixon*, 418 U.S. 683 (1974).

of the case in the lower courts—i.e., the case need not have been decided or made the subject of an order. In this instance, finality is not a prerequisite of review. Similarly, appeal is not limited to " 'those final judgments which terminate an action . . .' but rather the requirement of finality is given a practical rather than a technical construction."[30]

The procedure of review in federal appellate courts does not involve a new trial but rather a review of the record from below —the facts, procedures, evidence, conclusions, and supporting opinion, if any, of the trial court—amplified and clarified by oral explanations and arguments before the appellate tribunal, as well as by written statements of arguments and supporting legal references (known as "briefs") submitted by counsel.

Stated simply, then, a court exercises "original" jurisdiction when a case is tried before it for the first time and "appellate" jurisdiction when it reviews the record of what another and lower court has done. Courts of equal status and authority in the federal judicial system, except in very rare instances, do not review the actions of one another. A court may, however, exercise original and appellate jurisdiction in turn at different times according to the nature of litigation brought before it. Among the regular constitutional courts only the Supreme Court of the United States combines both types of jurisdiction to a significant degree.

Jurisdiction of the U.S. District Courts. The jurisdiction of these courts is wholly original, and they are trial courts *par excellence.* They may hear and decide, or otherwise dispose of, cases and controversies arising under the whole array of federal law stemming from the Constitution, from laws made in pursuance of it, or from treaties of the United States. As was noted above, some of their jurisdiction, like that involving "diversity" suits between citizens of different states, is shared with the courts of the several states, but significant portions of it are both originally and exclusively assigned to the District Courts. Thus, original exclusive jurisdiction includes prosecutions arising under the postal laws and regulations, admiralty and maritime matters, patent and copyright laws, proceedings in bankruptcy, disputes growing out of the capture of prizes of war, and, in general, all prosecutions based upon national law defining crimes against

---

30. *Eisen* v. *Carlisle & Jacquelin,* 417 U.S. 156 (1974), quoting *Cohen* v. *Beneficial Loan,* 337 U.S. 541, 545–546 (1949), with reference to 28 U.S.C. section 1291.

the United States. The jurisdiction of these tribunals is wholly controlled by Congress, which can grant to or withdraw from them whatever jurisdiction, either original or appellate, it sees fit, subject only to the restraints imposed by the jurisdictional provisions of Article III. These courts also share responsibility for enforcing the orders of some government departments and agencies, and in some instances review their actions. But since that review is not of facts found or of rulings on points of law made by a *court of law*, it still can be said that the United States District Courts have no appellate jurisdiction.

To summarize, the jurisdiction of District Courts can be expanded or curtailed at the will of Congress, and they can be given appellate authority. Ninety percent of their decisions are final, even though it is possible for the losing party to have at least one review by a higher court as a matter of right if he can afford it and desires to proceed further.

In addition to these arrangements, Congress has provided a special "fast track" to the Supreme Court for certain cases that otherwise could get there only by going the regular route through the Courts of Appeals. The technique, based on statute and Supreme Court rules, is not often used, and when used is seldom successful. It consists of bypassing the Court of Appeals by either side's petitioning the High Court to take jurisdiction on review, following action by a District Court judge.

The Justices are known to be reluctant to short-circuit the established judicial mechanism by permitting an action to go around one of its main components. They have made clear their expectation that the procedure will be invoked only on behalf of matters genuinely of "urgent public importance" requiring "immediate" settlement by the Supreme Court, and they have consistently discouraged attorneys from trying to bypass the intermediate appellate tribunals. The process is available, however, for resolution of major public issues when, for example, time will not admit delay; or when the Courts of Appeals have had ample opportunity to go over the legal ground, have made their contributions to the record, and cannot be expected to add enough to justify the delay (perhaps as long as three to five months) involved in going to them.

In spite of the obstacles impeding easy recourse to it, the bypassing route to Supreme Court review has been utilized to handle some of the nation's most urgent public law questions. It was employed to call up key emergency measures of New

Deal era legislation. It was used to consider and turn down the habeas corpus petitions in *Ex parte Quirin*[31] of five captured Nazi saboteurs landed by submarine on American shores in World War II. It was used to end the national coal strike in 1947, to formulate a sweeping interpretation of the war powers,[32] and, more recently, in the Pentagon Papers case.[33]

Jurisdiction of the U.S. Courts of Appeals. Standing in something like a pyramidal relationship to the more numerous District Courts are the eleven United States Courts of Appeals. Their jurisdiction, like that of the District Courts, is completely determined by Congress, and their authority and functions are almost wholly confined to those of an appellate nature. Except for a few opportunities for direct appeal from the final decision of a District Court to the Supreme Court, any final action taken by a District Court may be appealed to the Court of Appeals of its circuit.

The Courts of Appeals review decisions reached by certain regulatory agencies, by the special courts of the territories, by certain courts of the District of Columbia, and by the Tax Court of the United States. Also, when called upon, they enforce the orders and review the orders and actions of certain administrative agencies of the executive branch of the national government. Even though the exercise of review power over rulings of regulatory commissions can be thought of as the exercise of original jurisdiction, it is only arguably so, and leaves the preponderance of the work of these courts appellate in nature.

Only about ten percent of the actions disposed of by the District Courts in fiscal 1973 (13,329) went to the Courts of Appeals, and of that number approximately one percent were accepted for review by the Supreme Court of the United States. The numbers make it clear that litigants who have had their day in the lower federal trial and appellate tribunals find their pathway to the High Court seemingly traversed by a wide and deep chasm. According to the statutes, this chasm may be crossed on appeal by right only if the dissatisfied litigant has relied in the Court of Appeals on a *state* statute held by that court to be repugnant to the Constitution, laws, or treaties of the

31. 317 U.S. 1 (1942).

32. *Woods* v. *Miller*, 333 U.S. 138 (1948).

33. *N.Y. Times* v. *United States* and *U.S.* v. *Washington Post*, 403 U.S. 713 (1971).

United States. Moreover, if appeal by right is open to him and he elects to use it, a litigant cannot later invoke the High Court's discretionary review power.[34] Seemingly, then, if he invokes one route of access to the Supreme Court from a Court of Appeals, he automatically closes to himself the only other existing one. But the severity of this constraint is much abated by the fact that since the time Fred Vinson was Chief Justice, the Supreme Court has been treating appeals in much the same manner as it does petitions for writs of certiorari. An appellant who seeks review by right is required to file not only a notice of appeal but also a jurisdictional statement explaining why the case belongs in the Supreme Court. All nine Justices vote individually whether to take the case, but on the affirmative votes of four Justices the Court will retain it. Appeals and petitions for certiorari now stand on essentially the same footing.

If appeal by right is not available, any party to a civil or criminal action may, before or after judgment, seek review by the Supreme Court by petitioning it to grant a writ of certiorari. Because there is no right to have the request granted, the Court may respond on its own terms, but if in the exercise of its discretion it consents to the petition, the effect of the writ is to cause the record of the proceeding to be brought up to the Supreme Court from the lower tribunal. However, issuance of the writ does not mean that the petitioner will get the satisfaction he seeks from the High Court. Writs of certiorari are not easily obtained, for, as was noted previously, in fiscal 1972 only 5.7 percent (134) of those requested (2,322) from the Courts of Appeals were granted. Neither the opportunity for direct appeal nor petition for a writ of certiorari seems, therefore, to present an easy path to review by the Supreme Court of the United States.

Rarely does a case go up from a Court of Appeals by the third available route: certification. A Court of Appeals may certify to the Supreme Court "any question of law in any civil or criminal case as to which instructions are desired, and upon such certification the Supreme Court may give binding instruc-

---

34. 28 U.S.C. section 1254 (2). Appeal by right is based on statute. The Supreme Court must take jurisdiction of a case brought to it on appeal by right, but it does not have to hear argument on the case or decide it on its merits.

tions or require the entire record to be sent up for decision of the entire matter in controversy."[35]

Jurisdiction of the U.S. Supreme Court.   Though primarily an appellate tribunal, the Supreme Court of the United States does possess constitutionally prescribed original jurisdiction "in all cases affecting ambassadors, other public ministers, and consuls, and those to which a State shall be a party." This original-jurisdiction clause has not contributed substantially to the Court's workload.

Congress has refined this clause to vest in the High Court *exclusive* original jurisdiction over suits between *two or more* states and those not in conflict with diplomatic immunity brought *against* foreign ambassadors or ministers assigned to the United States. But Congress has prescribed that the High Court share other matters of original jurisdiction with the lower courts.[36] The High Court *may* accept all actions or proceedings *brought by* ambassadors or other public ministers of foreign states or to which consuls or vice-consuls of foreign states are parties, all controversies between the United States and a state, and all actions and proceedings brought by a state against the citizens of another state or against aliens.[37] Nevertheless, the types of proceedings included in the High Court's original jurisdiction are few and are not often encountered. During the October term, 1972, only seven cases were disposed of under this jurisdiction.[38] In many terms, there is only one such case, and occasionally there are none at all.

It should be obvious from the foregoing account that the Supreme Court is set apart from the lower national courts by jurisdictional and procedural barriers. Its original jurisdiction is narrowly defined; rights of appeal are few in number and without assurance of High Court action; and its certiorari jurisdiction is wholly discretionary. These formal protections are essential in order to prevent the Court from being overcome by

35. 28 U.S.C. section 1254 (3). An example of this rarely used means of access to the Supreme Court can be found in the case of *United States* v. *Barnett*, 375 U.S. 805 (1963).

36. U.S. District Courts share concurrent original jurisdiction over cases brought by representatives of foreign governments, over some brought by the United States against a state, and over some initiated by a state against a foreign state, an alien, or citizens of other American states.

37. 28 U.S.C. section 1251 (b).

38. *Statistical Abstracts of the United States, 1973* (Government Printing Office, 1973), p. 159, table 259.

the business brought to it. The Court is saved only by the constraining effect of these protections and by its own ability to reject any case it does not wish to take. Many appeals are summarily dismissed "for want of a substantial federal question"; many others result in summary affirmance of the lower court's action based solely on the rationale of the case as set out in the jurisdictional statement and the briefs accompanying the appeal.

The relationship of the Supreme Court to the lower tribunals is largely a function of congressional power. A wide variety of statutes has been enacted, but, as with other subjects of legislation, every proposal to modify the Court's jurisdiction immediately becomes the object of political pressures. But this will be considered in a later chapter. Suffice it now to state that, subject to the realities of the legislative process and applicable constitutional restrictions, the appellate jurisdiction of the Court may be made to include whatever substance and procedures Congress may assign to it.

Regarding the appellate powers of the Court, more important than the statutory and constitutional provisions is what the Justices are willing to do at any given time with the discretionary control they hold over application of the formal rules and procedures. The Justices can make the Supreme Court as isolated or as accessible as they desire it to be, depending upon how they employ their discretion to take or to reject cases.

SUMMARY

The above specifications of jurisdiction determine which courts can entertain what types of litigation. As technical and dry as they may seem, these specifications define the heart of the formal relations that exist between the courts of the regular constitutional system in the national judiciary. In the operation of any judicial system one of the most fundamental considerations in the resolution of legal disputes by courts of law is the competence of the tribunal to act. If jurisdiction were not assigned to differentiate the authority of the various units of the system, it would be impossible to maintain order between them, to provide symmetry and consistency in the law, to obtain review, to rely upon the force of precedents in keeping with the principle of *stare decisis*, and to utilize most of the procedures long established within our system of differentiated courts. Every tribunal would have the same force and competence as every other; the determinations of each would be equal in authority to those of any other. Hence, the jurisdictional specifications that exist between the courts of the regular constitutional system largely govern not only access by litigants to the relief they can afford, but also the movement of litigation and other relationships between the tribunals themselves.

To think of these considerations solely in terms of statutory statements and formal rules of procedure is to miss their greatest significance. Courts are instruments of social control, operating in an atmosphere of legal formalism. The cases brought to them for resolution reflect the struggle within society of contending economic, political, patriotic, financial, commercial, religious, and many other forces. So also does the disposition of those controversies—in some instances conspicuously so. The expanded role of government in contemporary American life has been called into being by the emergence of forces only it can control, of conditions only it can ameliorate, of services only it can provide, of requirements of national security with which only it can cope. Yet, every new piece of legislation rolled out in the mills of the political system creates causes of litigation raising new questions for judicial solution. The solutions ultimately are controlled by judicial organization, intercourt relations, procedures, and personnel. The invention of special three-judge District Courts and the gradual expansion of their jurisdiction, the periodic creation of additional lower courts and the more common creation of additional judgeships, the establishment of Courts of Appeals in 1891, and the creation of the Supreme Court's discretionary authority by enactment of the "Judges' Bill" in 1925—to mention but a few examples—are the products of congressional efforts to adjust the established judicial structure to the pressing demands of practical necessity.

The judicial, as well as the legislative and executive parts of the government, responds to pressures within society. As the need is felt, the structure and rules of procedure governing operations of the Supreme and lower courts can be modified. Artful use can be made by the Supreme Court of its numerous types of broad discretionary power; access to its authority can be tightened or relaxed; recognition may be varyingly given to the social consequences of decision-making as determinants of legal principle; and judicial self-restraint or bold policy innovation can be the courts' carefully measured accommodation to the variable conditions of changing times.

Through the whole process runs a constant interplay between the courts and Congress. What answers can be given to serious conflicts of economic interests, how the rights of individuals are to be adjusted to the tensions and insecurities of modern life, who can attack oppressive laws in the courts and the circumstances under which it can be done, what types of relief can be provided, what tribunals can offer remedies, and a host of similar questions can be dealt with only as variables of legislation and rules. Sometimes congressional action is a response to a judicially initiated reform; in other instances it is stimulated by judicial discovery of a problem solvable only by statutory rule; occasionally it grows out of what amounts to an invitation to "legislate" extended to Congress by the judiciary; sometimes it is provided by judicial obstructionism. Time after time in the relations of the judicial and legislative powers, Congress has reacted to facilitate the work of the courts. On more rare occasions, it has also reacted to constrain the judicial power or to undo its effects or repudiate its rulings.

Whatever its source, much modern legislation breeds litigation, grist for the mills of justice. Legislation is social policy, creating rights and privileges, conferring benefits, and imposing obligations. It is usually the direct consequence of a need in society to reconcile conflicting demands or to allocate advantages seeking recognition and the backing of public authority. But because the translation of pressing needs into statutory form by legislative action is never perfect, the impact of policy controversies is not dissipated by the process or product of enactment. Instead, it is merely given another dimension, and thrust into another arena of control—that of the judiciary. Then—according to considerations of jurisdiction, discretion, formal rules and procedures, informal interpersonal and intercourt relations, and other, often undiscernible, imponderables—conflicts of interests are transformed by lawyers into lawsuits which become objects for the application of judicial power.

CHAPTER 3

The Lower Courts: Working Characteristics and Relations

Though incomplete, the hierarchical relationship between the Courts of Appeals and the District Courts within the respective circuits is closer than that between the inferior tribunals and the Supreme Court. Both Appeals and District Courts are litigant-centered, both deal with the same types of cases (although the questions brought to each are substantively very different), both are tied together by the trial-appeal relationship, and both operate in the knowledge that, except for a very few litigants, they provide a method for settling disputes that is self-contained. Moreover, the lower courts have primary responsibility for handling the litigation of private parties. That responsibility tends to set them apart from the Supreme Court, which, as we have noted, does not exist to guarantee justice in private litigation. Also, the ability of the High Court to supervise the lower courts, though supposedly considerable, is in practice less than is generally thought, for although it can reverse their decisions, the probability is small that it will have a chance to do so.

LOWER-COURT PROCEEDINGS

The District Court judge is so intimately related to the work of trial lawyers appearing before his tribunal that the best training for that bench may be experience as a trial lawyer. Such a background would certainly provide a judge with such desirable attributes as a practical approach to principle, knowledge of federal rules of civil and criminal procedure, a better understanding of lawyers and parties who appear before him, and a greater proficiency in promptly dispensing justice. In the opinion of Bernard S. Segal, onetime chairman of the American Bar Association's Standing Committee on the Federal Judiciary, "in the case of a vacancy in the United States District Court— a trial bench called upon to conduct the most complex and varied litigation—a lawyer to be considered must have a reasonable amount of trial experience, preferably at least some of it in the federal courts."[1] Trial experience can enhance a trial judge's confidence in his mastery of his craft, and it can better enable him to meet on a par the attorney who may try to mislead, buffalo, or overawe him. Perhaps no other preparation can do as much to familiarize a new judge with the methods and functions of a trial judge and with the demands that will be made upon him as a key participant in the coordination of law and facts.

That fewer than one-quarter of the Supreme Court's total membership had prior service in the lower national courts and particularly in trial courts must influence their attitudes toward the inferior courts and perhaps even toward inferior-court judges. These Justices cannot know, except through sympathetic participation in the experiences of inferior-court judges, the world of the lower courts and of lower-court judging. They have not "been there," and although having "been there" is generally conceded by a Justice to be of little value in the performance of his formal duties, the experiental gap can only contribute to the isolation of the lower-court judges from their counterparts on the Supreme Court.

The trial process often calls for a large number of subjective rulings. To be sure, many of them are incidental, but many others are of first importance. Such rulings arise from the framework of procedure governing both pre-trial and trial phases, and are apt to include at any time rulings on motions, requests for continuances, challenges to the admissibility of evidence, the issuance and use of process, the appearance and testimony

1. Quoted in S. S. Chandler, "The Role of the Trial Judge," 50 *ABA Journal* 126 (1964). More than one bill has been introduced in Congress to require federal trial experience as a qualification for appointment to the District Court bench.

of witnesses, rulings on relevancy, competence, and materiality, and a host of others.

Although he may take a ruling under advisement, in most instances, in order to avoid unduly delaying the course of the trial, the District Court judge must make a speedy ruling, without time for researching determinative standards. Knowledge of the applicable rules of procedure and of evidence is clearly essential, as is the ability to make quick, adroit use of them in practical application. The "working judge" must possess versatility and practical ability, whereas the appellate judge needs theoretical intellectual capacity that can be employed at his leisure in a quiet atmosphere of meditation and study.

The district judge may be a participant in an emotionally charged process with emotionally charged parties, and frequently with emotional interests at stake. The atmosphere within and without the courtroom may be one of surging unrest. The trial judge cannot lose sight of the fact that public confidence in the entire fabric of judicial administration begins at the grass-roots level where his court operates. At the same time, when there is no jury he must endeavor to make objective determinations of fact and of law. As are all other judges to some degree, the District Court judge is the prisoner of his impressions—impressions of testimony, of the character and credibility of witnesses, of attorneys and their courtroom tactics, of hidden purposes, and, indeed, of all the participants and their actions. Of all the judicial participants in the resolution of legal conflict, the trial judge is closest to the realities of the conflict.

In contrast, Appeals Court judges and Justices of the Supreme Court operate in a relatively serene atmosphere marked by marble, plush, drapery, dignity, calm, and orderly proceedings. Appellate-court activity is unmarred by volatile exchanges between counsel, by tearful and agitated witnesses, by badgering interrogation, by shouted objections, by pleas to jurors, and by instant rulings on objections and motions of attorneys. Decorum, formality, and deliberateness are the unvarying order: sensationalism, surprise, and turbulence are alien to the austere dignity of the appellate courtroom. Furthermore, appellate courts are far removed from the factual contexts of the cases they review. Only to the extent that an accurate impression of the facts can be conveyed in the trial record or brought home in oral presentation can the relative values of the arguments be determined.

It is out of rulings on the issues raised and motions of counsel made during trial that questions of a constitutional nature often arise—particularly questions pertaining to the procedural or substantive rights of an accused person. Some such questions, of course, are presented by the parties as substantive issues on which the litigation is based. Many are settled immediately by the trial judge and are never heard of again, but some supply the bases of subsequent appeals. Those answered by a trial or intermediate-appellate court may be as difficult and as important as those for which Supreme Court review is sought and granted. Although it is customary to say that questions brought to the High Court from below are the "most difficult" or the "most complex" problems of constitutional or statutory law, what is probably more accurately meant is that their selection by the nation's highest tribunal lends them an air of importance that many of them lacked when first decided below. The Supreme Court has the last judicial word on them, but all have been ruled upon by at least one lower court and were no less "difficult," "complex," or "fundamental" at that time.

Although he has some discretion in the way he applies them, the trial judge spends much of his career enforcing technical and procedural rules about which there is little disagreement. Thus, at most times the rules and standards of his craft hem him in and constrain his exercise of judgment. Occasionally, however, he may have a chance to resolve a landmark question of first instance, and then he can exercise discretion akin to that of an appellate judge in choosing between alternative interests. This was the case with Judge Merhige in his capstone decision recognizing constitutional rights of prison inmates and their right to due process of law—a decision that gave recognition to a whole new arena of rights and to a wholly new legal status of prisoners. It was also true of Judge John J. Sirica's unique order to President Nixon to produce specified evidentiary materials needed for the Watergate investigation and litigation. Other examples include Judge Joseph C. Waddy's decision barring an executive veto imposed while Congress was in recess; Judge Orin G. Judd's order that the bombing of Cambodia be halted, thus negating the authority of President Nixon to wage war; and Judge William B. Jones' order directing the executive to cease impounding appropriated funds necessary for carrying out statutory objectives determined by Congress.

LOWER-COURT OPINIONS

A federal trial-court judge usually does not write lengthy opinions in the manner of an appellate judge. Only if he presides at trials of very important issues or public policies is a lower-court judge apt to write out in detail the reasons behind his decision. If, however, the judge sits without a jury, he is required by the Rules of Procedure to "set forth the findings of fact and the conclusions of law which constitute the ground" of his decision. This rule does not today give the trial judge as much shelter as it once did, for the use of juries in U.S. District Courts has been noticeably declining. The decline has been particularly apparent in the trial of civil controversies.

The parties most interested in what a district judge has to say are the attorneys and the parties to the litigation at bar. Although the immediate assumption might be that a judge's opinion is written to explain to them what conclusion of law was reached in their case and the reasons upon which it was based, viewed from a different perspective these are not the only parties to benefit. The federal trial judge must be conscious that his opinions will serve the interests of other lawyers and litigants as well. He must address his opinions to the needs of the trial lawyer of the future who will be researching precedents. From this perspective, it is important that his opinions be clear and precise statements of facts and issues of law. They should show skillful analysis and an expert handling of legal authorities, answer those contentions of counsel regarded as meritorious, and state the conclusion so that it cannot be misinterpreted. By logical, persuasive, and rigorously reasoned argument the trial-court judge must justify his conclusions in a manner that will gain respect for him and acceptance for them.

There is, of course, a fundamental difference between the nature and purpose of a trial-court opinion and that of a reviewing court. The trial judge is deciding one or more specific questions of law, sheltered by the knowledge that the dissatisfied litigant has a right to appeal. His opinion, then, is addressed mainly to the parties at hand and is intended to inform them about the considerations that influenced his judgment.

An appellate-court judge, on the other hand, cannot direct his opinion to the lower court alone. The intermediate appellate judge must look both ways, to the trial court below and to the Supreme Court above. The appellate opinion, therefore, must address the issue disputed on appeal, explain its resolution to the trial-court attorneys and litigants, and at the same time try to gauge the reaction of the High Court. To no little extent, the appellate opinion is a set of instructions to the lower tribunal, and includes within its paragraphs standards not only to guide the lower court in disposing of the case at hand but also to guide all lower tribunals regarding disposition of all future similar cases.

THREE BROAD CATEGORIES OF LOWER-COURT CASES

Cases coming before the District Courts can be separated into three broad classes based on their respective importance in the relations between lower courts and the Supreme Court.[2]

In the most numerous class are cases of a private type in which the issues, the applicable law, and the consequences of solution are virtually devoid of broad policy implications. This class embraces actions arising out of torts, contracts, sales, negotiable instruments, etc. Here the economic, social, or political philosophy of the court is most unlikely to have a significant effect on the outcome. The only influences at play are those impossible to measure or to eliminate because they are always inadvertently present: the subconscious bias of a judge, the superior talents of one counsel, the ability of a side to make the evidence and facts work for it, the subtle advantages that wealth and community standing give a litigant. Legal maneuverings for advantage are of course present both openly and behind the scenes, but cases in this category are almost totally devoid of community interest or broad public policy implications: their outcome is of interest only to the immediate parties to the proceeding.

The second category of judicial business is more obviously public in nature, inasmuch as the public is directly involved as prosecutor (as in all criminal cases) or as a defendant (as in a civil suit against the government). But here, also, there is little probability that important policy determinations will grow out of the character of the litigation or the issues it generates.

2. This section is based largely on J. L. Blawie and M. R. Blawie, "The Judicial Decision: A Second Look at Certain Assumptions of Behavioral Research," 18 *Western Political Quarterly* 579 (September 1965).

Whatever extralegal influences there are in shaping the outcome usually take an overt form between the principals or their counsel or between one or more of them and a representative of the public authority. This category of litigation sometimes brings forth an exhibition of concern by spokesmen for interests not immediately involved as parties. It may be difficult to imagine concerted support by a national interest group growing out of a tort or contract action involving the federal government, but the criminal trials of Julius and Ethel Rosenberg generated widespread reaction and had important policy implications for the future.

Nevertheless, judicial business in this category rarely allows the presiding judge to escape the tight restraints of law and procedural requirements. Seldom does it give him an opportunity to exercise judicial discretion so as to make new law with novel public consequences. Occasionally, however, a lower-court judge is presented with a controversy in an area of law that is not developed, clear, or authoritative. Then his opportunity for constructive innovation may produce far-reaching consequences not only for the litigants but for all other members of the public who may in the future be affected by it. Even so, a judge in such a case is unlikely to make law pertaining to the structure, functioning, or powers of government or the relationship of individuals to public authority.

Few cases fall in the third category, but their impact is far-reaching and often dramatic in its consequences for the character of national life. This category embraces those actions, many of them deliberately brought for the purpose of attacking a public policy, that clearly and unavoidably raise novel questions of statutory interpretation or basic constitutional doctrine. Such actions, known as "test cases," may arise de novo. Or they may be created by a group (such as the NAACP) which converts an existing controversy brought by a private party for private ends into a vehicle for establishing precedent-setting doctrine having policy consequences for large numbers of people or interests.

Novel questions that arise in District Courts often originate in actions in equity for injunctive relief, or actions to obtain a judicial clarification of rights and duties in the form of a declaratory judgment. Others emerge collaterally from the main case, as events propel the judge of a District Court into a novel issue which he has no alternative but to decide as one of first impression. Thus, in about a dozen different cases in 1973–74, District Court judges ruled in quick succession that President Nixon did not have authority to impound federal funds appropriated by Congress; that he did not have authority to order dismantling of a statutory administrative agency and termination of its programs as long as Congress funded it; that in the absence of congressional authorization or declaration of war he could not on his own authority order military forces into combat in Cambodia or order the release of bombs over that country; and that the 1866 Civil Rights Act provision that "all persons . . . shall have the same right to make and enforce contracts as is enjoyed by whites" prohibited all-white private schools from denying admission to black participants. Each ruling was on an original question that had never been answered judicially. Finally, District Judge William B. Jones agreed to rule on the question of whether President Nixon could invoke his sweeping construction of "executive privilege" to prevent public disclosure of sixty-seven memoranda sought by plaintiffs in a consumer-interest action brought against the Department of Agriculture. The issue of "executive privilege" was thrust upon Judge Jones in a collateral fashion, but this did not make it less important for the Senate Watergate investigation and Office of Special Watergate Prosecutor, which were eager to gain access to other materials denied them on the grounds of executive privilege.

Thus only a few cases growing out of categories two and three bring the lower courts into contact with the Supreme Court in matters of general public significance. This is because they affect the structure or functioning of the government, or the rights and duties of the individual vis-a-vis the public authority or the acts of its agents. These are the cases that are of elementary importance to the nature and operation of the constitutional system. They shape its character and reassure its membership or sometimes, unhappily, unsettle its tranquillity.

With respect to these few cases, lower-court judges are political actors, but their position in the judicial process relegates them to the supporting cast. In cases raising basic public policy issues the starring roles are reserved for the members of the Supreme Court. The lower courts are placed by their inferior status and its historically consolidated constitutional position at a great disadvantage in any contest with the High Tribunal. And yet even in these few cases of fundamental doctrinal importance the lower courts are able to evade, avoid, or convert the mandates of their judicial superiors and to impose upon the "uniform" principles of Supreme Court doctrine their diverse localized interpretations and applications. We shall shortly see how they do this.

However, except within a limited geographical area and in a disjointed manner, in these matters neither type of lower tribunal can serve as the conscience of the people, as the Supreme Court is said by many of its students to do. District Courts rarely enjoy the prestige necessary to overcome the many local, regional, or national consciences that exist. A district judge cannot make his vision of a constitutional ideal the standard to which the rest of the nation conforms; he can only serve as local spokesman for such values and can win acceptance only to the extent that he can overcome contrary local consciences. He cannot impose upon the country a standard of uniformity that overrides the diversity and individualism traditional in American life. Achievement of these objectives is beyond the ability of the discrete lower tribunals, individually or together, to attain.

LOWER-COURT DISCRETION

Although *stare decisis* is supposed to constrain judicial independence, lower-court judges possess considerable discretion in resolving the issues that come before them. In cases presenting broad policy questions this discretion is virtually unlimited. Judges of inferior courts will find among the precedents in the 421 volumes of Supreme Court *Reports* relatively few that sharply constrict their freedom of choice. They are just as free as higher-court judges to pick and choose among the available alternative principles of law which compete for acceptance, and to select those they deem appropriate and applicable. On occasion, some of them have blithely ignored clearly controlling precedents because they disagreed with the implications for public policy. The interstices of decisional law are as numerous and as large for lower as for higher tribunals. Nevertheless, judges below cannot ignore with impunity what those on the level next above them have said or may say, for to depart radically from (or totally ignore) precedent is to invite appeal and probable reversal. The nature of the judicial process demands that the inferior courts be governed by the requirement of unity and a semblance of uniformity within the system of law. It is only according to the amount of brashness, judicial astuteness, or courage felt at the moment that they play with precedent within the limits of plausibility. A Supreme Court precedent, perhaps more often than is popularly realized, means to no little degree only what a lower-court judge is willing to concede that it means.

The breadth of discretion available to inferior courts is largely attributable to the way in which High Court opinions are expressed. Going beyond such obstacles to precise communication as the multiple meanings of many words of common usage, legitimate misunderstanding, deliberate misinterpretation, and disrespect below for the persons and attitudes of current Justices, what a lower-court judge does in response to a High Court order may be influenced largely by the meaning he derives from the mandate. His construction depends upon the clarity of instruction from above. The less clarity there is, the greater opportunity there is for him to read meaning into the message from his judicial superiors.

The constraint imposed on lower courts fluctuates according to case and judge and is affected by a variety of considerations, among which the following ought to be considered.[3]

If the decision above is an innovative one, one that breaks ground in an unexplored area of constitutional or statutory exegesis, the lower courts probably have greater freedom to interpret its meaning than if the latest decision must be construed in the context of previously decided questions. Rarely does a case in a controversial area of public policy set forth a clear and comprehensive rule of law. In fact, judged by results produced through the decades, the Supreme Court's preferred practice is to prescribe vague rules, accompanied by equally vague standards governing their application to the facts defining particular situations of future controversy.

Sometimes a lower court cannot know with certainty what led the High Court to its decision. Can the court below determine whether the decision grew out of *all* the elements that defined the litigation or only of selected ones? Did the High Court deliberately leave the ruling unconfined because the case was perceived in its broadest social dimensions? Was the rule

---

3. This subject is treated extensively in Richard Johnson, *The Dynamics of Compliance* (Northwestern University Press, 1967), pp. 61f.

formulated above intended to be limited only to the facts and issues immediately pertinent to the case at hand? What *were* the facts of record, what was their force, and what issues of law or considerations of social policy were immediately pertinent? Did the opinion above obfuscate its rule by *obiter dicta*, by dragging into its scope elements not relevant to the immediate conflict and its resolution? Was the ruling made with clarity but in a manner that invites political or legal action to modify or refute it? Was the opinion made open to varying interpretations by an excessively narrow focus on the facts and issues? Or was it rendered vague by its failure to formulate a precise rule that can be adhered to with reasonable fidelity? The Supreme Court provided a particularly flagrant example of this last instance in the obscenity cases and in applying the "clear and present danger" rule. In doing so it set a vague and shifting standard by which lower courts and other affected parties were expected to gauge and apply the protective force of a basic constitutional freedom.

Certain phrases often found in High Court opinions virtually invite the inferior courts to duck their imperative force. Qualifiers such as "In the case before us" or "On the facts at hand" may save for the High Court maximum flexibility in differentiating the case being tried from any similar future case; but such restrictive language reduces the precedential force of the decision, increases lower-court uncertainty, and helps lower courts to escape the binding power of the decision by distinguishing it on the facts from a subsequent case.

Walter F. Murphy has pointed out various ways by which the lower courts of the federal judiciary can evade or avoid the effect of the High Court's decisions.[4] The discretion available to a lower court when it gets a case back on remand for "further consideration" is, of course, extensive. All things considered, the phrase, "further proceedings consistent with this opinion," often used when the Supreme Court sends a case back down, does not seriously tie the hands of lower courts. Occasionally, however, there are somewhat more specific and detailed instructions. Ambiguities of language, gaps in reasoning, divergent reasoning expressed in concurring and dissenting

---

4. "Lower Court Checks on Supreme Court Power," 53 *American Political Science Review* 1030–1034 (1959).

opinions, deliberate avoidance of issues—all these contribute to the area of discretion in which lower-court judges may roam.

More elusively but no less typically, the Supreme Court has rested its conclusions upon its reading of the lessons of history where there is no authoritative, unequivocal evidence to support its assertions. It has relied upon assumptions which a majority asserted had been always held, as though its assumptions created law by virtue of the majority's out-of-hand remark to the effect that they did so. It has gone on mind-reading excursions into the intentions of the Constitution's framers, reconstructing these intentions admirably to reinforce the majority's position at hand. In order to suit the present need it has reached conclusions by extending a documented fact or attitude beyond its original scope and context. It has drawn dicta from prior opinions and cited them in later cases as authoritative statements of legal principle, ignoring the original form and place of the utterance now cited as precedent. It has relied on assumptions allegedly supported by the statutes or decisions of the era—assumptions that in fact were debatably contemporary in time or applicable in subject. The Supreme Court's use of adventitious asides, non sequiturs, specious or unsupported conclusions, oversimplifications, and hand-tailored history contributes greatly to the flexibility available to inferior courts. And this, in turn, enhances the independence of the lower courts and diminishes their actual subordination to the Supreme Court.

Uncertainty has been compounded by the Court's willingness to disregard its precedents. Although the Supreme Court has never been regarded as firmly bound to its prior decisions by *stare decisis* in matters of constitutional principle, such inconsistency contributes to the consternation of inferior-court judges concerning the status of affected principles of law. Thomas Jefferson made such complaints about the Supreme Court under John Marshall, and similar criticism was directed against the Court under Chief Justices Taft and Hughes.

In sum, uncertainty occurs below whenever lower-court judges are confronted by the Justices' inability or disinclination to give precise and comprehensive detail to the guidelines by which their standards are to be implemented. Refining statutory and constitutional mandates by judicially including and excluding later cases from their application hardly promotes clarity of understanding and certainty of application by inferior courts.

Even making the generous and highly unrealistic assumption that all lower-court judges want to receive and faithfully follow directions from the Supreme Court, the lower-court judges often cannot be certain what principle has been enunciated. Trial-court judges are disadvantaged by the Supreme Court's apparent readiness without forewarning to enter new areas of decision, to repudiate or modify a recently established precedent, or to abandon precedent without admitting it has done so.[5] The poor quality of many of its opinions adds little to the efforts of the lower tribunals to find clarity and exactness in its determinations. Consequently, the lower courts and their bars are too often left with inadequate guidance for coming to grips authoritatively with pending cases. Thus the exercise of discretion, often leading to departure from precedent and the striking out on a new course of doctrinal development, remains the only path open to them.

The lack of constraint upon lower courts ascribable to these factors, and to others soon to be reviewed, makes myth of the proposition that precedent in fact has commanding force upon lower courts. It also explodes the belief that *stare decisis* robs them of discretion in their application of Supreme Court decisions to current cases. The rule of precedent can mean for lower-court judges only that as a practical matter they *ought not* lightly and for insufficient reason to depart from the prescriptions of higher authority.

---

5. *The U.S. Reports* abound with countless examples of the Court's unpredictable or obfuscating actions leaving lower-court judges in doubt. Thus *Barron* v. *Baltimore*, 7 Peters 243 (1833), has never been explicitly overruled. *West Virginia State Board of Education* v. *Barnette*, 319 U.S. 624 (1943), reversed *Minersville School District* v. *Gobitis*, 310 U.S. 586 (1940), only a short time after the latter was decided. The array of opinions and decisional grounds in *Youngstown Sheet and Tube Co.* v. *Sawyer*, 343 U.S. 579 (1952), defies comprehension and almost guarantees that the decision will never have great force as precedent. *Erie Railroad* v. *Tompkins*, 304 U.S. 54 (1938), suddenly repudiated, almost wholly without warning signs of an impending shift, a doctrine of approximately one hundred years' duration. *In re Sawyer*, 124 U.S. 200 (1888), established the doctrine that equity may not enjoin a criminal prosecution, but exceptions subsequently admitted to the law have so eroded its application that little of its substance remains. In the face of these and myriad other uncertainties, the inferior courts operate "subordinate" to the Supreme Court. See Blaustein and Field, " 'Overruling' Opinions in the Supreme Court," 57 *Michigan Law Review* 151 (1958); W. O. Douglas, "Stare Decisis," 4 *Record of the Association of the Bar of the City of New York* 152 (1949).

LOWER COURTS AND LACK OF PRECEDENTS

A wholly new dimension of the relations between lower courts and the Supreme Court is broached when the question is asked "What should a well-meaning trial- or intermediate-court judge do when he is confronted by a wholly new situation for which the Supreme Court has provided no reasonably analogous precedent?" The lower-court judge is then able to write on a clean slate in much the same way that the Supreme Court does when constitutional interpretation carries it into a new realm of principle. In such circumstances the lower judge has no discernible constraints on his discretion other than those that are always applicable to the judicial function. The question is not whether he ought to break new ground, for he may have no choice but to do so.

Lower courts can generate power for themselves *vis-a-vis* the Supreme Court by decisions, especially in aggregate, that extend its precedents into new areas of application. Such decisions tend to force the High Court to rule upon questions which it avoided in the past and, if left to its own wishes, would continue to duck in the future. The High Court can probably escape more easily from passing on an isolated issue raised in a single case than it can duck one upon which numerous tribunals below have ruled. All the same, it has demonstrated notable ability to withstand concerted pressure from below.

As an example of their power in this area, lower courts extended the principle of *Brown* v. *Topeka* to prohibit *de jure* segregation in public parks, swimming pools, beaches, golf courses, and other facilities not explicitly comprehended by the initial decision.[6]

These courts also derived from *Brown* and its postscript a constitutional principle requiring busing of school children to obtain a judicially acceptable racial mix in neighborhood public schools that were segregated *de facto*. In 1971, the Justices agreed that a school district could be compelled by lower courts to bus school children within a single independent school district in order to offset *de facto* residential segregation.[7] For the next four years, however, it resisted strong pressure to determine

6. *Brown* v. *Topeka*, 349 U.S. 294 (1955).
7. *Swann* v. *Charlotte-Mecklenburg Board of Education*, 402 U.S. 1 (1971).

the constitutionality of busing across school-district lines and also across political boundaries of cities and counties as ordered by many lower courts across the country. Finally, on July 25, 1974, it drew the line by ruling that, except when the absence of black children from suburban schools could be proven to be the result of deliberate acts of discrimination, lower federal courts could not order transportation of school children across political boundaries. The Court's ruling seemed to be a clear reaction to the lower courts having pushed the issue too far.[8]

As Professor Murphy points out, it is in this nebulous area of transitional constitutional law that lower-court judges find the greatest peril in the shifting sands of doctrine, for they must try to ascertain how far the higher court is willing to go and the rate of change it is willing to tolerate. To exceed either limit is to invite reversal. The lack of clear guides leaves open to the lower judge, however conscientiously objective he may try to be, a choice between what he *believes* the future line taken above will be, what he *hopes* it will be, and what he believes it *should* be.[9] He thus is drawn into a judicial guessing game the outcome of which may be determined by nothing more than the willingness and ability of a dissatisfied litigant to make an appeal to higher authority. If the lower judge adheres too rigidly to existing precedent or if he too freely anticipates the future course of decision above, he risks being repudiated on appeal. He probably ought not to oppose a discernible line of developing doctrine while it is being refined by higher authority. In such times he can prudently follow in the higher tribunal's wake, abide by established principles, and leave to authority above, particularly to the Supreme Court, responsibility for clarifying shifts of doctrine. This the higher courts do by overruling their own precedents whenever they are disposed on their own initiative to do so. Probably most judges in the lower federal courts both lead and follow higher authority as conditions of time and circumstances suggest is desirable, though an occasional adamant refusal to follow along *does* occur because of mere disagreement with the decisional trend indicated from above.

The willingness of several hundred minds to break new ground

8. *Milliken* v. *Bradley*, 418 U.S. 717 (1974).

9. Walter F. Murphy, "Lower Court Checks on Supreme Court Power," 53 *American Political Science Review* 1028 (1959).

of public policy, consider new alternatives, and experiment with new solutions in order to obtain results can be highly instructive to the nine Justices of the Supreme Court and also to the Congress, which may even be impelled by the decisions of lower courts to take legislative action. That same willingness of lower-court judges to innovate public policy, however, can inject into constitutional doctrine an excess of diverse and perhaps conflicting interpretations which complicate the task of the intermediate and Supreme Courts. The intermediate courts can bring about uniformity within their respective circuits, but only the High Court can do so on a national scale.

Whenever the Supreme Court evades a really thorny issue, preferring to leave it unanswered, lower courts must bear the burdens they themselves have created.[10] In such cases the lower courts must carry the responsibility of laying out some preliminary doctrinal boundaries, taking the brunt of criticism, and permitting the High Court to evaluate the practical consequences of their efforts at definition and implementation. In such important areas of conflict as motion-picture censorship, loyalty and security activities, pornography and obscenity, reapportionment, congressional investigative powers, and, of course, busing, the Supreme Court, for some time before it finally stepped in, seemed willing as long as possible to leave the resolution of these issues to the lower courts. Finally, however, it did intervene to mitigate the uncertainty and confusion that its silence had permitted to develop.

To some extent, the trial and lower appellate judges *ought* to take the initiative to dispose of cases which break new ground. To some extent they cannot escape doing so in the normal discharge of their duty. Some, also, will do so out of a spirit of adventure or out of personal convictions. Perhaps, therefore, the only question is how far they should gratuitously inject themselves into controversial fields of constitutional doctrine or novel public policy in which neither higher judicial authority nor the political branches have given clear directions. For this question there is no easy answer.

10. See Harper and Rosenthal, "What the Supreme Court Did Not Do in the 1949 Term," 99 *University of Pennsylvania Law Review* 293 (December 1950). Similar articles for subsequent years can be found in vols. 100, 101, and 102.

LOWER-COURT RESISTANCE TO
HIGH-COURT GUIDANCE

Although lower-court judges are subordinate to the Supreme Court, they are also participants with it in an articulated system of judicial administration. The result is that as subordinates they are expected to give deferential treatment to the High Court's determinations of law which, in lawyers' lingo, are *res judicata*. As participants, on the other hand, they sometimes act as critics of the Court's determinations and occasionally express their opposition both inside and outside their courtrooms.

"Off-bench" criticism by lower-court judges has long been recognized as part of legitimate intercourt byplay. Criticism from lower-court judges may influence higher-court doctrine, produce legislative responses, affect popular acceptance of doctrine, or even stimulate overt disobedience by the affected public, other judges, or executive personnel. The assumptions are, of course, that off-bench expressions of disagreement will not transgress the standards of professional propriety, and that higher-court decisions will be implemented by lower-court judges however disaffected they might feel. Neither assumption, however, has always been found to be true.

Even lower-court conferences and councils on occasion have taken the initiative in opposing Supreme Court decisions. They have done this by such means as petitioning Congress to enact legislation modifying the High Court's determinations. The Judicial Conference of the District of Columbia sought to induce Congress to vitiate the force of the "Mallory Rule" by which the Supreme Court narrowed the admissibility of confessions obtained during police interrogation of suspects in the District of Columbia. The Judicial Conference of the United States has several times recently endorsed legislation to negate High Court decisions. Lower-court judges sometimes testify before congressional committees in opposition to the decisions of their superiors. In a survey of 351 lower-court judges regarding the state chief justices' 1958 criticism of certain Supreme Court decisions, *U.S. News and World Report* found that, of the 128 who responded, 59 approved of the criticism, 50 disapproved, and 19 refused to express an opinion. In courtroom statements and in opinions, lower-court judges can always make known their dislike of the rationale of particular High Court decisions.

They can also deplore the consequences inflicted by the decisions upon society.

In spite of their formal position of subordination to the Supreme Court, judges of inferior tribunals possess ample opportunities and many means both inside and outside the courtroom for registering opposition to High Court precedents or orders. We have already discussed a lower court's discretion in following, distinguishing, or ignoring precedent. Many additional opportunities arise when cases carried to the Supreme Court for review are sent back to the lower courts for final disposition or continued action. In this way, the lower courts have the final crack at broad public policy and constitutional doctrine formulated by their judicial superior. They are able with impunity to ignore or defeat policy directives from above, and they can undermine the efforts of the High Court to instill homogeneity into the substantive law. In fact, the lower courts' use of their means for remonstrating, resisting, or retaliating may well be another factor for the Supreme Court to evaluate in reaching its conclusions. Decisions between alternatives certain to precipitate adverse reaction below and others that would not are quite possibly weighed in the seclusion of the conference room.

Since the Supreme Court is most unlikely to invoke its powers to mandamus a lower-court judge or to coerce him upon threat of contempt, it has no effective weapon by which to discipline a judicial subordinate seriously. A judge who opposes its decisions and is supported by strong prevailing local sentiment is not likely to find himself in much difficulty. He need not resort to overt hostility and defiance, as many modes of indirect evasion are available. Criticism, sharp and unmistakable, finds its way into lower-court opinions; judges on remand can "distinguish," "qualify," "limit," or "confine" a precedent to the precise facts that called it into being. Judges can evoke a countervailing principle of equal merit, or follow precedent so exactly that extreme, unanticipated, and undesirable consequences will result, leading to reversal or modification of the precedent above.

TACTICS OF DISTRICT COURTS TO DEFEAT SOCIAL POLICY: AN ACTUAL INSTANCE

The following account of the attempt of James Meredith to obtain justice in a District Court of the deep South illustrates what an unsympathetic judge can do under the influence of localism. At the time of his effort to gain admission to the University of Mississippi, Meredith petitioned the District Court of the United States for the Southern District of Mississippi to grant a preliminary injunction against the admitting officers of the school. This was in order to aid all blacks, not himself alone, in seeking admission.

Judge Mize was not in sympathy with integration. The date he set for the hearing on Meredith's petition was so late that it delayed and temporarily defeated the purpose of the injunction. Once begun, the hearing was constantly interrupted by Judge Mize in order to accommodate "other court business"; continuances were granted on highly dubious grounds at the request of the university officials; and additional recesses of court were taken. When at last the hearing was concluded, there was a prolonged delay before the judge rendered his decision denying the relief sought.

The conduct of the hearing and the preparation of the record were so badly handled in the District Court that on review the Court of Appeals, Fifth Circuit, found that the "muddy record" defeated the appellate court's effort to determine whether legitimate reasons existed for the university's refusal to admit Meredith. The Court of Appeals indicated its concern over the manner in which the hearing below had been handled. It also indicated how the proceeding should be conducted. It took exception to five of Judge Mize's prior actions: (1) engaging in practices that prevented introduction of valuable evidence into the record, (2) taking an unduly permissive attitude toward the white university officials, (3) constraining unduly Meredith's interrogation of witnesses, (4) restricting his arguments, and (5) limiting his introduction of evidence. The appellate court also stressed a number of specific evidentiary deficiencies of the trial record that resulted from the way Judge Mize conducted his court. And it pointed out the error committed when the trial court limited the introduction of evidence to that pertinent to the narrowest possible interpretation of Meredith's challenge to the university officials.

Judge Mize, however, was little daunted by such criticism. When the action came back to his court on remand from the Court of Appeals, Judge Mize ignored the strictures and directions of the opinion above. With some show of greater dispatch than had previously been exhibited, the trial court dismissed

Meredith's complaint on the ground that there *were* reasons other than the matter of the petitioner's race which justified his exclusion from the University of Mississippi. Again, the Court of Appeals reversed Judge Mize. Determined still, Judge Mize then obtained from sympathetic Judge Cameron of the appellate court four stays of the remand, three of which Judge Cameron's colleagues vacated. The fourth stay was set aside by Supreme Court Justice Hugo Black. Only then did Judge Mize bow to superior authority and issue the injunction, but the relief it granted was confined by its terms to Meredith as an individual only, not to blacks as a class as Meredith had sought.[11]

OTHER TACTICS OF JUDICIAL OBSTRUCTIONISM

Examples of nonconformity by lower-court judges are sufficiently numerous to make it clear that their subordinate status is not a fully effective curb on unpredictable behavior. District judges, and to some extent appellate ones as well, do sometimes respond to the influence of their local backgrounds. But it is clear that most judges most of the time strive to overcome that influence. Probably no judge has been wholly the captive of local background and pressures. That lower courts jump when the Supreme Court says "frog" or that inferior courts follow after their superior in parade-ground order are but two frayed strands in a threadbare theory.

Without question, many legitimate reasons exist for delays in the proceedings of lower courts. But those that occurred during many civil rights cases in the lower federal tribunals of the South seem to numerous observers to have been artfully purposive, originating in the unwillingness of some trial judges to give disciplined, timely compliance to the orders of higher courts. In some circumstances the time factor is so important to the standing of the plaintiff or to the adequacy of the remedy he seeks that its extended lapse can render the issue moot or frustrate his effort to obtain relief.

In addition to the tactics employed by Judge Mize in the Meredith proceeding, other means of delay and obstruction are available. Some District Courts have dismissed civil rights cases

11. Recounted in comment, "Judicial Performance in the Fifth Circuit," 73 *Yale Law Review* 90 (1963), at pp. 91–92.

on the dubious ground that they were not class actions as they were presented as being. Other courts have refused to act until what they regarded as determinative issues of state law had been answered by the highest state judicial authority. Such a procedure has often meant a delay of one to two years until a state supreme court could be consulted.

Instances can be found when abstention was employed wholly without foundation by federal trial or appellate judges, whereas in others the issues were clearly controlled by settled precedents that were ignored or distinguished below. An artful judge may ignore established authority in formulating his determination of the results, thus inviting almost certain appeal, reversal, and remand—and the lapse of still more time. And if a hostile trial judge correctly estimates that the plaintiff's time, resources, or determination are running out, one more dilatory tactic may carry the issue by forcing the plaintiff to abandon his action. The possibility of this latter result is what in part impels organizations and groups to back legal action.

The attitudes publicly adopted by District Courts in their highly localized settings have had significant impact upon the local reception given to Supreme Court decisions. The way District Courts go about carrying out higher-court mandates and applying policy can do much to set the tone of local response, as can the public statements of the judges. If all Southern district judges had tried to explain more clearly to disaffected populations the bases of judicial actions, their efforts might have brought about a higher degree of willing compliance.[12] The demeanor assumed by a lower court provides a means by which it can, in effect if not by design, be subtly engaged in a sapping operation while giving a seemingly good-faith discharge of its duty. Any propensity in this direction is bound to be heightened in direct proportion to the emotional force of an issue, for what arouses one judge's ire may leave another unmoved. The covert techniques are ready and waiting to be used on any occasion by a lower-court judge who yields to his personal reaction or to the forces of local pressure, thus subordinating his obligations as judge, federal officer, and agent of the law.

Conversely, long-term resistance can only be undertaken at a price, for the Supreme Court *does* reinforce the lower courts

12. Blaustein and Ferguson, *Desegregation and the Law* (Rutgers University Press, 1956), pp. 223, 224.

by legitimating their actions.[13] Their status, prestige, authority —in a word, their effectiveness in the public-law realm as courts—depends in part upon the favor in which they are held above. Their effectiveness is dependent also upon the existence of a supporting public consensus which their continued wholesale opposition to the High Court's rulings could go far to impair. Hence, their opposition may not be pushed too far.

LOWER COURTS AND THE CONGRESS

The political impact upon lower constitutional courts is not limited to the non-legal inputs which bear on the decisional process. Inferior-court decisions, individually, or more likely in the aggregate, may stimulate congressional legislation of a supportive or restrictive and even punitive character. The legislative product may be directed solely at the lower tribunals, but it also may be aimed at the exercise of the judicial power *in toto*; in either contingency, the effect usually bears directly upon the relationships of the lower to the higher courts.

Legislative action is most frequently aimed at the Supreme Court,[14] but when doing so would serve some political purpose Congress seems not the least reluctant to draw a bead on the lower tribunals also. The reapportionment issue at least twice caused the District Courts to become enmeshed in congressional reaction to a judicially created imbroglio.

The first instance occurred in August, 1964, when Congress reacted in a dramatic and unusual fashion to express its disapproval of the Supreme Court's handling of six reapportion-

13. Schubert, *Judicial Policy Making* (Scott, Foresman, 1965), pp. 66–67.

14. For example, S. 2646, 85th Congress, 1st Session, known as the "Jenner Bill," would have withdrawn the appellate jurisdiction of the Supreme Court over certain cases dealing with subversion, cases involving admission of persons to the bar by a state, and cases growing out of actions of congressional committees. This particular proposal was apparently not aimed at the lower national courts. Students who wish to pursue this subject further should consult R. Berger, *Congress Versus the Supreme Court* (Harvard University Press, 1969); A. C. Breckinridge, *Congress against the Court* (University of Nebraska Press, 1971); W. F. Murphy, *Congress and the Court* (University of Chicago Press, 1962); C. H. Pritchett, *Congress Versus the Supreme Court* (University of Minnesota Press, 1961); J. R. Schmidhauser and L. L. Berg, *The Supreme Court and Congress: Conflict and Interaction, 1945–1968* (Free Press, 1972).

ment cases the prior June. The House of Representatives passed a bill to take from District Courts jurisdiction to hear suits brought against existing state legislative apportionments. The bill also denied the Supreme Court authority to review any lower-court determination in an apportionment case.[15] Concurrent Senate reaction took the form of a proposed amendment to the U.S. Constitution to permit states to depart from strict regard for equality of representation based upon population. A filibuster ended that strategy, but another strategy was adopted urging but not commanding District Courts to allow states up to six months to implement a federal-court reapportionment order. It passed the Senate but died when the House failed to enact it.

The second instance occurred when Congress cut the District Courts out of important proceedings under the Voting Rights Act of 1965. It provided that political subdivisions subject to the statute could gain exemption from its operation only by demonstrating to a three-judge court in the District of Columbia that no racial discrimination in voting had been permitted within the petitioning jurisdiction. Normal practice might have employed the appropriate District Court within the requesting state as the most competent and informed agency to grant the exemption. Instead, Congress chose to eliminate the District Courts and to use in their place a special court wholly removed from local interests and pressure. In too many instances District Court judges had been unwilling carefully to examine allegedly offensive state laws and practices and had failed to apply with vigor and dispatch the protections of civil-rights statutes. The Voting Rights Act provision also amounted to congressional criticism of the Supreme Court's failure to obtain full-faith compliance from the lower tribunals in their discharge of statutory obligations. It was acknowledgment by Congress that High Court supervision was inadequate for the tasks at hand.

Congressional reaction can be much more devastating to "normal" operations and intercourt relationships than the above two efforts intended. Had the 1957 Jenner Bill[16] become law, decisions of lower (and state) courts affecting internal security,

15. This measure was lost in the Senate when its consideration was passed over. See *Congressional Quarterly Guide to Current American Government* (Washington, D.C.: Congressional Quarterly Service, 1966), pp. 27–37.

16. See note 14.

segregation, congressional investigation, national employee security regulations, and federal preemption would have been freed of judicial review by the Supreme Court. Applications of constitutional doctrines in those areas as determined by Courts of Appeals or by the highest state courts would have thereafter been final. Had the proposal become operative, the Supreme Court's function of harmonizing national law by reviewing and controlling decisions of lower tribunals would have been transferred to Congress, where the full force of political influence could be brought to bear upon efforts by statute or constitutional amendment to deal with the affected subject areas. Lower-court judges disposed to do so might have been tempted to regard the curbing action by Congress as an *invitation* to them to go their independent ways to the full extent of the freedom conferred. Some might even have regarded it as a *directive* from Congress to do so. And whatever the constitutional proprieties of such congressional action might be, it would have behind it the lurking, ominous portent of legislative retaliation against lower tribunals whose future actions might be displeasing.

Congressional legislative action can obfuscate the substance of active law and force the lower courts to serve two masters at once. Such was the case when Congress reacted to *Miranda* v. *Arizona*.[17] This decision held that before a person in police custody can be interrogated he must be informed that anything he says may be used against him, that he may remain silent, that he has a right to counsel and to have counsel present during interrogation, and that if he cannot afford counsel, counsel will be appointed for him. Congress' enactment of the 1968 Crime Control Act[18] flatly contradicted the doctrine of *Miranda* and antecedent decisions by permitting federal trial-court judges to admit into evidence "voluntary" confessions made by persons who had not been informed by detaining officers of their rights to be assisted by counsel and to remain silent.[19] Trial-court judges hence found themselves forced to serve two masters at once with knowledge that *no action* could satisfy both. Thereafter, federal inferior-court judges were confronted by the dilemma of whether to observe and implement the law as built

17. 384 U.S. 436 (1966).

18. Omnibus Crime Control and Safe Streets Act, 1968, 90th Congress, 2nd Session.

19. H. J. Abraham, *Freedom and the Court*, 2nd ed. (New York: Oxford University Press, 1972), p. 126.

up in decisions of the Supreme Court, their judicial superior, or to follow the contradictory rule of the statute enacted by Congress, their political superior. The controlling section of the law, enacted under Article III and the "necessary and proper" clause of Article I, Section 8, Clause 18, was of questionable constitutionality. The possible invalidity of the statutory rule was admitted by its legislative proponents, but the Senate Committee on the Judiciary justified its having created the dilemma on the grounds that the High Court often reversed itself, that *Miranda* was decided by one vote, and that by the time the constitutional question could be resolved by litigation, the Supreme Court, in the Committee's opinion, would have swung around to the statutory position. In the meantime, of course, lower courts were forced to choose between the statutory rule in anticipation of a judicial shift by the Supreme Court, and the existing constitutional rule laid down by their judicial superiors, for the rule of precedent made it binding on the courts below until that shift from *Miranda* actually took place.

THE TRANSMISSION OF SUBSTANTIVE LAW

The staying power of the rule of precedent can be explained not only by the traditional rationale but also on a pragmatic basis. Of course the durability of this principle in American legality is due partly to the conventional justifications in theory offered on its behalf and partly to the historical transfer of common-law origins to the western shore of the Atlantic. These contributions account for its origin, just as law-school instruction in the case method and in the taught virtue of *stare decisis* in part underlie its preservation. The contention here is not that these factors play no role; it is only that a very large part of the role of precedent in our judicial system is *not* due to a traditional regard felt by lower courts for decisions of their judicial superiors.

And yet attorneys are trained to think and act as if this were true. This is because attorneys desire to win their cases for their clients, and they feel they have a better chance to win and to be sustained on appeal if they invoke the authority of an established rule. Particularly at the appellate level the mechanism of judicial administration is geared to the necessity of their doing so. Appeal to precedent is an appeal to the tried, the known, the proven—in other words, to the comfortable security of the past rather than to the uncertainty of change. Reliance upon precedent at trial is tantamount to persuading the judge that there is safety in relying upon what has been previously accepted, perhaps less likelihood of reversal if appeal is taken. Pragmatically considered, reliance on precedent is clothed with respectability derived from the wisdom of other judges and from the prestige of higher authority and of age. Hence citing of precedent by counsel is at least as much a device for securing victory in the courtroom as it is an appeal to higher values inherent in a legal system dedicated to preserving social order, progress, and justice. The broader ends of society, however, rarely if ever induce counsel to advocate and support by precedents a position contrary to the interests of the client, who, after all is said, is endeavoring to win. All of which, if valid, further weakens the authority and binding force of precedents upon lower courts.

Litigants, lawyers, and lower courts, therefore, may be thought of as consumers of Supreme Court decisions. But how are Supreme Court decisions communicated to lower-court judges? Are special distributional arrangements necessary? Are decisions available in printed form only, or is there distribution of meaning orally by means of conferences? Or is their meaning only to be arrived at by inference? What mechanism is provided to ensure uniformity of understanding by 400 District Court and 97 appellate judges to guard against honest distortion through misunderstanding? As noted above, communication rests primarily upon common-law techniques of researching and citing precedent, the superior binding force of Supreme Court decisions, and the Supreme Court's supervisory power over lower courts. It rests to a far lesser degree upon explanations conveyed in conferences and councils. In the last analysis it rests on a system of self-education, free interpretation, and voluntary compliance by lower-court judges.

A number of practical problems complicate the transmission of meaning. The understanding of lower courts is hampered by the many disparate problems concurrently brought to them for resolution; by the press of litigation on the lower courts; and by the necessity for lower courts to filter out the meaning of a case from the factual and substantive factors surrounding it. Comprehension is further hindered by the oftentimes conglomerate character of Supreme Court releases, including perhaps a dozen decisions with opinion and a hundred or more memorandum opinions released on a given day; by the necessity to analyze each result in the context of its total milieu; and by the fact that one dramatic opinion may so overshadow all the rest that it obscures them, whatever their relative importance might be.

According to Richard Johnson, the court system itself—that is, the formal structure of courts—constitutes "an important channel through which a ruling is transmitted to those who are directly under obligation to act."[20] Judges of lower courts not directly affected by disposition of a case above may or may not be inclined to acquaint themselves with all the High Court has to say or with the consequences of its various dispositions. Rarely is a case pending below affected by today's decision above. Thus, judges of inferior courts may await receipt of official reports and library resources before undertaking to acquaint themselves with the latest decisions from on high. Perhaps their principal means of being brought up to date is the efforts of other parties—namely, attorneys appearing before them whose arguments and citations at trial or in briefs on review endeavor to educate the court to *all* established precedent and law favorable to their legal positions. Some education in precedent takes place in conferences and councils, and at least one Court of Appeals routinely distributes copies of its decisions to all other Courts of Appeals.[21] But in the last analysis, there is no consistent method by which lower federal-court judges are uniformly informed about the meaning and intended effect of Supreme Court decisions.

If such a method were found, could it accomplish much? Could it curb use of the avoidance techniques available to judges who do not wish to follow what they understand to have been meant above? Could it overcome the ambiguities, omissions, imprecisions, and divergences of thought common in many opinions above? Could any method of transmittal make automatic judges' knowledge and acceptance of Supreme Court rulings and also eliminate the impact of localism upon Supreme Court decisions? Probably not.

20. *The Dynamics of Compliance* (Northwestern University Press, 1967), p. 61.
21. Court of Appeals, Second Circuit, according to Karlen, *Appellate Courts in the United States and England* (New York University Press, 1963), p. 55.

JURISDICTIONAL VARIATION IN NATIONAL LAW

There is abundant evidence that national lower-level courts exercise such latitude of discretion in so many matters that judicially determined policy varies discernibly from one jurisdiction to another and from one level to another. The disconcerting fact prevails that national law is not nationally uniform. The constitutional guarantee of an independent judiciary may well cause lower-court judges to feel a tendency to exercise a truly independent judgment on all matters within the authority of their respective tribunals. It may make them feel that to escape being subservient minions of higher courts, to fulfill their sworn duty, they would fail the system should they forgo expressing disagreement with such higher court decisions as their independent judgment led them away from. And all the while they would be professing fullest possible respect for higher authority. For judges below to conclude thus would be a natural, if not inevitable, consequence of their positions within the judicial system and of the processes and characteristics of judicial decision-making.

From the structure and character of the national judiciary it follows that the exercise of judicial power within the system cannot be unitary and uniform. Each lower court, each judge, is a discrete power center in the system, and to assert that Supreme Court decisions are fully adhered to and that national law on any given subject is uniform throughout the United States would stretch credibility to the breaking point. These centers of power are subjected to and respond in different ways to diverse pressures and may shape law for their jurisdiction in sharply or subtly opposing directions. They may do so even in the face of a presumptively binding decision of the Supreme Court. Mr. Paul Sanders has affirmed how, as a government attorney, he learned to speak of the "law of the Fourth Circuit" as different from the "law of the Sixth Circuit" albeit derived from the same national statute. It was more disconcerting to find that "the Laws" of a single statute might also vary between District Courts, and even between judges of the same court, in a single state, despite extensive Supreme Court interpretation.[22]

22. P. H. Sanders, "The Warren Court and the Lower Federal Courts," Unpublished paper quoted in John R. Schmidhauser, *Constitutional Law in the Political Process* (Chicago: Rand McNally, 1963), p. 425.

These realities of the judicial interrelationships between national constitutional courts are such as to cause Richardson and Vines to conclude that in spite of some supervision by the Supreme Court, and in spite of some elements of hierarchy present in the judicial structure, integrated and coordinated national law does not emerge from the federal judicial system. Not only can the Supreme Court not adequately supervise the decisions and personnel of the lower federal courts, but the judicial-council movement, which seeks integration of judicial activities, has neither the power nor the resources to perform this function. In many instances, local views of national law prevail through decisions of District Courts, and these views are unchecked, and even supported, by regional courts. National values and national law become shaded by a variety of local behaviors and values inherent in the one-man decisions of District Court judges.[23]

To account for this condition is not an easy task. Most studies of the decisional behavior of inferior-court national judges find the cause in forces of localism which condition the selection of the judges and which they cannot wholly escape during their tenure. Other causes are often found in the personal backgrounds, preferences, biases, and other subjective influences conditioning the responses of judges.

But Professors Carp and Wheeler have added another dimension to the explanation and decisional variation among lower courts.[24] They concede the influence of the usually recognized variables that are "slow to release their grip" on a newly appointed judge. But, addressing their attention to the question "Why do U.S. trial judges in a given district continue to behave differently from those in other districts and in other circuits?" they propose that "there is an additional and perhaps theoretically more compelling explanation for the behavior in question." They say that "differences in the judicial behavior of the U.S. trial judges from region to region may be explained to a large degree by the socialization process *after* they become judges."[25] The principal judicial agents of judicial socialization are reported to be the new judge's more experienced peers,

23. Richardson and Vines, *The Politics of Federal Courts* (Little, Brown, 1970), p. 175.

24. Carp and Wheeler, "Sink or Swim: The Socialization of a Federal District Judge," 21 *Journal of Public Law* 359 (1972).

25. Ibid, p. 362.

especially those in service with him on the same court. The chief judge often assumes central responsibility for breaking in a novice member of his court. But Carp and Wheeler turned up the interesting but not surprising fact that appellate-court judges play a minor role as socializing agents. Their geographical inaccessibility, the personal "distance" generated by their superior judicial positions, the risk of impropriety (real or imagined) inherent in contacts between trial and appellate judges, hostilities growing out of felt caste structure, and sensitivity to the argument that "Only another trial judge could understand the problems of a trial judge"[26] help account for the gulf separating district and appeals-court judges.

However, the gulf can be narrowed when all district and appeals judges in a circuit convene for meetings of the circuit's judicial conference. The panels assembled, papers read, and discussions held help bring lawyers, administrators, judges, and law teachers together for reciprocal education on problems of general interest to the lower judiciary. Introductions made and personal contacts established in the informal atmosphere that generally characterizes conference proceedings ease later efforts to obtain assistance in solving problems, for judges seem most reluctant to turn to unfamiliar colleagues for aid or advice. Therefore, much value is derived from the fact that the circuit conference brings together new and experienced trial judges from the entire circuit area, broadens their range of contacts, and provides a significant opportunity for overcoming the gap between them and the circuit appellate judges (and—when one or more attends—between themselves and Justices of the Supreme Court). So, in the last analysis, the conferences can serve as important agents of judicial socialization by enhancing contacts between judges and by imparting information to them. In so doing, the conferences add another dimension to the articulation of the judicial structure.

26. Ibid, p. 378.

CHAPTER 4

The District Court Judges: Conditioning Factors

The process for selecting judges of the District Courts is a diffused and politicized process that permits entry of diverse participants. The impact of politics, both party and non-party, upon the choice of district judges contributes to their differences of outlook and their separation from the appellate courts. It also feeds their spirit of localism. The influence of particular interests and pressures probably contributes nothing to the selection of well-qualified personnel for the benches; yet it is a potent force to be reckoned with. Judicial selection is a process eagerly participated in by Senators (and occasionally by Representatives), by the American Bar Association's Committee on the Federal Judiciary, by agencies of the executive branch, and by numerous other parties with political motives who would like to shape the outcome. The interested involvement of these parties, their debate over methods of judicial selection, and their struggles to gain or prevent a particular nomination reveal concern for the results produced. All recognize that the recruitment process brings values to the federal bench which, because of lifetime tenure, attain a semi-permanent status there.

The active interest exhibited in federal judicial vacancies should occasion no surprise, for District Court judgeships are highly attractive positions. Few lines of professional endeavor have a higher social status than does service on the federal bench. And few offer greater opportunity to exert authority and influence over the affairs of men. Moreover, the District Court judge rules over a judicial fiefdom, for he is subject to no real hierarchical control of a close and continuous type. The district judge has great authority and autonomy of operation within his court, and he can do much to set the tone of his judicial district. He can influence, and perhaps even determine, the constitutional philosophy of his district on important issues of public policy. And he can set in motion events and chains of litigation generating change-making social and political action or reaction.

Because impeachment as prescribed by the Constitution is the sole available (and wholly inadequate) means for removing unacceptable judges from office, the initial choosing of the best-qualified personnel is of prime importance. Nevertheless, recruitment is accomplished by what amounts to a wholly political arrangement. This is not to suggest that there is anything inherently undignified in procedures of a "political" nature. But when judges are selected according to whom an aspirant for nomination knows, how much influence his backers can mobilize in his support, whether he belongs to the "right" political party, or whether the party owes him an obligation for services rendered, such considerations seem to be too "political"—whether that term refers to "who gets what, when, and how" or is limited to narrow partisan politics.

THE JUDICIAL SELECTION PROCESS

The same recruiting process operates for selecting all federal judges, and involves many actors in a wide variety of roles. Our purpose is to examine those phases of recruiting District Court judges that may have an impact on intercourt relations. Hence, we shall limit attention to certain aspects of American Bar Association, senatorial, local political, and judicial involvement in the selection of federal judges.

A brief account of the process will indicate where these actors fit in. On its face, the formal process is very simple, consisting of nomination by the President, the giving of advice and consent (confirmation) by the Senate, and appointment by the President. In fact, however, the process is complex and cumbersome and involves a wide variety of actors who play many different roles. The real process probably never works the same way twice: unique combinations of support and opposition develop around each aspirant and nominee. And in addition to the President and Senate, the actual process normally involves individual Senators, the Department of Justice and the FBI, the American Bar Association's Standing Committee on the Federal Judiciary, the Senate Judiciary Committee, local and state political and professional participants, and sometimes federal judges. All participants in the process bring different perspectives to it and seek to accomplish different ends. The selection of a federal judge comes out of the diversity of influences and counterpressures which define judicial recruitment.

The Influence of "Senatorial Courtesy."   The selection of District Court judges affords a rich source of patronage and is subject to the practice of "senatorial courtesy."[1] Because the District Courts are superimposed on the states, the recruitment process tends automatically to be captured by the states' political forces. A United States Senator, especially of the President's party, in whose state a federal District Court vacancy occurs can ordinarily be relied on to urge upon the President the names of one or more "deserving" individuals. These names may be drawn from among the Senator's friends or from persons to whom he owes political obligations; or they may be recommended to him by state, county, or municipal bar associations, state or local political party chiefs, important interest groups, government officials, or other sources of influence within the Senator's state. When "courtesy" operates, the President normally yields to the necessity for consultation and cooperation, and presidential horsetrading may then become the order of the moment. This is preferable to risking defeat of an unsupported nominee at the hands of united senatorial opposition backing up the objection of one of their own members. Moreover, political reality often will dictate that a President extend to his "friendly" enemies of the other party rights of cooperation and consultation in matters of judicial selection.

The Senate's role in deciding upon a nominee for a District Court judgeship imposes tight constraints upon the President's freedom of choice. If the President ignores the proprieties of senatorial courtesy, he can expect a hot fight with one or more of his own party's members in the legislative chamber and the almost certain defeat of his candidate by the Senate as a whole.

1. On the role of the Senate see J. P. Harris, *The Advice and Consent of the Senate* (University of California Press, 1955).

He will almost certainly alienate the Senators whose personal selections he ignores and may lose votes needed for enactment of administration measures. The constitutional requirement that the Senate give its advice and consent to judicial nominations has been converted into Senate domination of the selection of district judges.

The Influence of the ABA. The appointing process also tends to become politicized because there is no agreement about the qualities a "good" judge should possess. The American Bar Association's Committee on the Federal Judiciary purports to be concerned only with securing quality appointments to the federal bench, but unmistakable ideological concern often masquerades as attention to "judicial temperament," "sound legal training," "good character," or professional achievement of the nominee. According to Glendon Shubert, ABA evaluations of nominees' qualifications amount to an expression of their standing in the legal profession.[2] Hence, the phrase "good judge" can be defined to accommodate any point of view that happens to suit the diverse parochial interests that bear on the selection process. Samuel Krislov suggests that ABA influence is properly focused on lower-court appointments because the qualifications for a lower-court judge are of a technical type that the ABA Committee is suited to evaluate.[3] The influence of the ABA probably helps prevent the appointment of the worst-qualified nominees, but it gives no assurance that the best-qualified ones will be appointed. Nevertheless, the committee has established a tight working relationship with the Department of Justice when nominations to the District Courts are under consideration.

Political Influences. Many District Court judges come from routine political backgrounds of the type earned at the state and local levels of American government. Some have been notable legal scholars and outstanding lawyers, but a successful career in practical politics is the most common path to the federal trial bench. Many district judges owe their positions to support from the dominant political forces in their state. The best gambit for a judicial hopeful is political activity on behalf of successful

2. *Judicial Policy Making* (Scott, Foresman, 1965), pp. 15, 16. On the role of the ABA, see J. Grossman, *The Politics of Judicial Selection* (John Wiley & Sons, 1965).

3. *The Supreme Court in the Political Process* (Macmillan, 1965) p. 19.

senatorial or presidential candidates. Another is holding a party chairmanship of a key county or state.

Government attorneys have better than normal access to trial-court appointments. H. J. Abraham states that the ABA Committee on the Federal Judiciary prefers nominees to have had at least fifteen years of legal practice.[4] Experience handling the government side of cases falling within District Court jurisdiction familiarizes government attorneys with not only the substantive law involved but also with federal procedures. Also, the high visibility of upper-level government counsel and Department of Justice lawyers may bring them to the attention of appointing or other influential parties and give them an important head start in the selection process. Moreover, upper-level government attorneys are frequently politically active people who joined the staff of the Justice Department or other agency, and most district judges have also been politically active.

Interest groups or other associations, particularly those having or likely to have litigation pending before the court involved, undertake to influence the appointment of district judges. The Southern Christian Leadership Conference actively championed the appointment of more blacks, and women's organizations urge the appointment of more women. State, local, and federal bar associations play important roles in the filling of vacancies, as do deans and other law-school figures, and non-legal professional, business, clerical, and other spokesmen for the community also play their part.

Judicial Participation in Judicial Staffing. Intercourt relations, too, are involved in the recruiting process. Judges may divide over the merits of a nominee, and their reactions do not always have equal force. The reaction of a respected judge may offset that of one or more less prestigious judges. And judicial influence over judicial recruitment is a two-way street, with lower-court judges sometimes influencing appellate-court nominees and appellate judges seeking to shape lower-court selections. Richardson and Vines state that "The members of the sitting judiciary seldom intervene in the selection process by directing attention to legal qualifications of nominees";[5] but enough instances of intervention based on other qualifications

4. *The Judicial Process*, 2nd ed. (New York: Oxford University Press, 1968), p. 28.
5. *The Politics of Federal Courts*, (Little, Brown, 1970), p. 67.

have occurred to suggest that judicial involvement in the re-cruiting process is more common than is suspected.

No roles have been formally set to permit judicial input, nor has practice regularized and legitimized a procedure of evaluation and endorsement. Nevertheless, intercourt relations may be affected by the fact that lower-court judges voluntarily or on invitation from the President, senators, and the Department of Justice make inputs concerning the qualifications of nominees to the federal bench. Chief Justice William Howard Taft solicited the views of judges J. W. Warrington and Henry Severens about Horace Lurton and Willis Van Devanter.[6] Chief Justice Warren E. Burger while an appeals-court judge apparently formed a close working relationship with Attorney General John Mitchell by virtue of which he made recommendations regarding advancement in the lower courts as well as to the Supreme Court. In April, 1969, he sent names to the Attorney General, purportedly at Mitchell's request, to give his "observations on district judges and others [sic] over the country who might warrant consideration for appointment or promotion on their professional qualities." He continued, "I enclose three names for the present and will be able to add others from time to time."[7]

The extent to which lower-court judges were involved in the senatorial politics of recent Supreme Court nominations has come to light through enterprising newspaper reporters. In a joint communication, all of the judges in the Fourth Circuit supported the ill-fated 1970 nomination of Judge Clement Haynsworth to be an Associate Justice of the Supreme Court. Similarly, all the judges of the District of Columbia Circuit supported Judge Warren Burger when he was nominated to be Chief Justice. And when the Chief Judge of the Court of Appeals, Fifth Circuit, wrote an effusive letter of endorsement to Senator Eastland, chairman of the Judiciary Committee, praising the qualifications of his colleague, Judge Homer Thorn-

6. See Walter Murphy, "Chief Justice Taft and the Lower Court Bureaucracy: A Study in Judicial Administration," 24 *Journal of Politics* 453 (1962), and A. T. Mason, *William Howard Taft, Chief Justice* (Simon & Schuster, 1965). Other episodes are recounted in Richardson and Vines, *The Politics of Federal Courts*, pp. 66–68.

7. From the *Washington Post*, 13 June 1974, pp. 22, quoting from a letter from Judge Burger to Attorney General John N. Mitchell, 4 April 1969.

berry, to be an Associate Justice, it was reportedly endorsed by all members of the court. Nevertheless, the nomination failed to gain approval.

After the Haynsworth nomination was rejected, President Nixon, determined to teach the Senate a lesson in response to its brash action, submitted the name of another strict-constructionist Southern conservative. His choice was Judge G. Harrold Carswell, a lackluster former district judge of limited experience who then sat on the Court of Appeals, Fifth Circuit. The efforts of Carswell's supporters to involve lower-court judges in the struggle to win Senate approval were intricate, and they may have been counterproductive. Only ten of the fifteen active judges sitting with him on the Fifth Circuit Court endorsed his qualifications. The lack of support from his circuit colleagues damaged him, but the failure of highly respected Judge John Minor Wisdom to endorse him, and also former Chief Judge Elbert P. Tuttle's revocation of his endorsement, probably hurt more. All three circumstances seriously weakened his senatorial supporters during the long fight that finally led to rejection of his nomination. After newspapers took notice of his circuit colleagues' lack of support, 50 of the 58 active District judges and 7 of the 13 senior district judges sent a statement to the White House: "The undersigned . . . endorse your nominee, Circuit Judge Harrold Carswell, as being well qualified to serve as associate justice of the Supreme Court."[8] White House release of this message was viewed as an effort to offset allegations that his professional peers did not respect Judge Carswell.

But involvement of district judges went beyond that statement. An organized effort was made to mobilize the help of friendly district judges to obtain a recorded endorsement of the Carswell nomination from their peers. Judge Daniel H. Thomas successfully solicited endorsement from all active and senior district judges in Alabama and Mississippi; at the request of Senator Russell B. Long (D., La.), Judge E. Gordon West sought support from his peer judges in Louisiana. But Judge West was turned down by two on the grounds that the activity was not proper. Fifth Circuit Judge Bryan Simpson, a friend of Carswell, contacted District Judge Albert Henderson, who agreed to canvass his colleagues in Georgia, while Judge Charles R.

8. Reported in the *Washington Post*, 5 April 1970, p. 1, col. 1.

Scott performed the same service in Florida.[9] But in the end the effort was to no avail.

However much value such suggestions and participation may have for a President and his Attorney General who need to staff the judiciary, the history of judicial involvement suggests the potential for both good and bad inherent in it. Should a lower-court judge, even upon invitation, try to influence the selection of a Justice who may later review his decisions? Conversely, should a Justice (Chief or Associate) participate in any way in the selection of lower-court judges? When a Supreme Court nomination comes down from the White House, should Senators induce support from judges and their active participation in mobilizing peer support? Should judges engage in an overtly political process with a strong partisan flavor?

In sum, the process by which federal District Court judges are selected is a very loose one, one that is virtually devoid of constraining constitutional and statutory standards. Fully open to the free play of partisan politics, it is subject to many pressures, great and small. At no point does it assure that a dispassionate, objective appraisal of qualifications for judicial office will be made.

Conformity and Diversity in Judicial Backgrounds. The judicial selection process admits a large number of aspirants who bring diverse qualifications into the nominating arena. In spite of this fact, those who gain appointment to the District Court benches share a number of common characteristics that presumably shape the performance of their judicial duties. Most judges are white, male, middle- to upper-middle class Protestants. Increasingly, however, the lower-court judiciary is coming to embrace all segments of American society, although blacks and other ethnic minorities and women continue to be underrepresented. Most District Court judges were born, raised, educated, and professionally trained in the state in which their court sits[10] and are assumed to have absorbed the local outlooks, attitudes and values. Most have been politically active at the state or local level, and an overwhelming proportion (98 percent) practiced law before ascending the district bench. More than 50 percent practiced on behalf of a public agency or were employed in other than private practice.[11]

9. Reported in the *Washington Post*, 5 April 1970, p. A2, col. 2.
10. Richardson and Vines, *The Politics of Federal Courts*, pp. 71, 72.
11. Ibid., pp. 75–78 passim.

All this is not to say, however, that the local origin of a judge will necessarily be reflected in his decisions. But participants in the judicial selection process often behave as though they believe background shapes performance on the bench. Why else, it might be asked, do Senators and other locally-oriented participants in the recruiting process emphasize local nominees? What other consideration would account for the high degree of political sensitivity that characterizes the appointment process? Why do presidential selections tend to favor nominees with a federal-government orientation, and why do they so consistently reflect the President's party affiliation and ideological persuasion? Suffice it to note here that a number of studies have shown positive correlations between judicial backgrounds and decisional patterns, a fact that seems to bear out the assumption that appointing authorities can ignore background factors only at their peril.[12]

Bloc Appointments. There is much to suggest that lags between social values of lower-court judges and those of society at large may be far more extensive than has been suspected. One antidote generally available and often invoked to solve this problem is to increase the number of lower-court judges, making as sure as possible that the new appointees will reflect the prevalent contemporary attitudes on questions of social significance. When Congress by statute creates a bloc of new judgeships, Presidents try to perpetuate the political influence of their administrations beyond their term of office by means of appointments they make to lower courts. If George Washington's selection of good Federalists to fill judgeships created by the Judiciary Act of 1789 is counted, politicking with the judiciary is as old as the Union. One of the first *overt* instances of politicking with judicial appointments came in 1801 with Federalist attempts to "reform" the inferior judiciary and make of it a safe bastion of Federalist principles. Two measures created 59 new judicial positions, which outgoing Federalist President Adams undertook to fill with deserving and loyal members of his party.

The inferior courts have continued to be the subject of periodic, thinly disguised efforts to realign their outlook by increasing the number of judgeships. For example, after the

12. See notes 15 and 19, this chapter, and Goldman and Jahnige, *The Federal Courts as Political System* (Harper & Row, 1971), pp. 64–77.

Wilsonian interlude in Republican control of the Presidency, Congress in 1922 gave to the impatient and patronage-hungry Harding administration 25 new judgeships. Waiting for normal attrition to produce vacancies in the judicial ranks to which loyal sons of the G.O.P. could be appointed was too slow. Hence, a Republican Congress provided some judicial manna, which the President distributed almost exclusively to deserving members of his own party. As expansion of the national judiciary continued during Harding's brief tenure and that of his successors Coolidge and Hoover, the total number of judgeships almost doubled. In 1952, after two decades of Democratic control and the appointment of almost two hundred Democratic judges, the Republican Party elected both a President and a Congress; the latter in keeping with tradition and sound politics created the judgeships for the President to fill. And in 1961, after six years of refusing to create them to be filled by a Republican President, a Democratic Congress established a bloc of 73 new lower-court judgeships close upon the election of a Democratic President. Glendon Schubert reports that these appointments were used by President Kennedy to bring about a new ideological outlook within the lower federal-court system.[13] In 1970 the Congress yielded to pressure from the judicial system and brought 61 new judgeships into being.[14] The filling of them by President Nixon continued into the middle of 1972.

It is the judicial system that suffers when a Congress of one political persuasion refuses to create judgeships to be filled by a President of a different persuasion. Increased caseloads brought on by growth of population and crime rates do not wait on the advent of ideological harmony between the White House and the Congress. Table 6 clearly illustrates the impact that political partisanship has had upon judicial selection in the past.

LOCALISM AND DISTRICT COURTS

Whereas the Supreme Court draws its legal business from federal courts of the entire United States, its territories and possessions, and in large measure from state judicial systems as well, the District Courts draw much of theirs from private law

13. *Judicial Policy Making* (Scott, Foresman, 1965), p. 67.
14. Omnibus Judges Bill, 84 Stat. 294 (1970).

TABLE 6

PARTISAN INFLUENCE ON THE CHOICE
OF ALL NATIONAL JUDGES

Appointing President	Democrats Appointed	Republicans Appointed	Others Appointed	% of President's Party
Cleveland (D)	36	—	1 (Indep.)	97.3
Harrison (R)	3	26	—	87.9
McKinley (R)	1	22	—	95.7
Roosevelt (R)	2	69	1 (Indep.)	95.8
Taft (R)	8	37	—	82.2
Wilson (D)	73	1	—	98.6
Harding (R)	1	43	—	97.7
Coolidge (R)	4	64	—	94.1
Hoover (R)	7	42	—	85.7
Roosevelt (D)	194	13	—	93.7
Truman (D)	128	13	—	90.7
Eisenhower (R)	11	178	—	94.1
Kennedy (D)	105	10	1 (N.Y. Lib.)	90.5
Johnson (D)	130	10	—	92.8

SOURCES: E. A. Evans, "Political Influences in the Selection of Federal Judges," *Wisconsin Law Review* 330–351 (May 1948), and H. J. Abraham, *The Judicial Process*, 2d ed. (Oxford University Press, 1968), p. 72. These sources disagree on the total number of appointees during the Harding-Hoover period: Evans shows a total of 161, Abraham 198. Abraham, *The Judicial Process*, 3d ed., p. 71, shows a party-consistency rate for Nixon's judicial selections of 93.7%.

litigation in small constituencies of fairly static character. In cases where district judges decide atypical questions having broad social consequences or far-reaching legal effects, an element of localism often is found in their views when those views are repudiated above.

The local orientation of District Court judges is inescapably in evidence, although its appearance varies with geographical region and with categories of issues. Kenneth Vines has reported that as of 1962, 51.3 percent of all Southern federal trial-court judges were born within their districts.[15] Moreover, 56.1 percent

15. K. Vines, "Federal District Judges and Race Relations Cases in the South," 26 *Journal of Politics* 337 (May 1964), at p. 348. See also Sheldon Goldman, "Characteristics of Eisenhower and Kennedy Appointees to the Lower Federal Courts," 18 *Western Political Quarterly* 755 (December 1965), at pp. 756f.

had attended law school in the state in which their district was located, and 89 percent had held government offices in those states.[16] In the Southern districts, the judges of federal trial courts tended to be "home born, locally trained and experienced." They were "closely related to their districts and could never be conceived of as 'carpetbaggers' by their severest critics."[17] He also reported that between 1954 and 1962 in race-relations cases before United States District Courts in the South, those district judges who had most experience in state and local government, who were closely tied to the indigenous sociopolitical ideology, and who presided over judicial districts containing a large number of black residents more often held against the claims of blacks. They most clearly reflected localism and employed obstructionist tactics to impede desegregation in "important and crucial" cases; across the board those same locally oriented judges were less favorable to black claimants than an objective adherence to Supreme Court policy determinations would have led them to be.[18]

In view of the fact that United States District Court judges are predominantly the products of local influences, ties, outlooks, identities, and local political organizations and support, these findings should occasion no surprise. Those ties and influences, especially as they affect the process for selecting district judges, have led Vines to conclude that although the selection and retention of federal district judges do not actually depend on popular choice, there is an obvious analogy to be drawn between the sources and nature of the close relationship binding them to their districts and those linking elected representatives to their constituencies.[19]

A District Court judge who is out of sympathy with an order

16. Vines, p. 343.
17. Ibid., p. 344.
18. Ibid., p. 345.
19. Richardson and Vines, *The Politics of Federal Courts*, p. 36. For a thorough analysis of social and political background factors associated with lower-court appointees of Presidents Eisenhower and Kennedy, see Sheldon Goldman (above, note 15), pp. 755–762. Goldman has also explored the complexities of the judicial selection process in "Judicial Appointments to the United States Courts of Appeals," *Wisconsin Law Review*, Winter 1967, pp. 186–214. A more general analysis of the appointing process with attention to the roles of specific players and to the combination of forces influencing its outcome is provided by Harold Chase, "Federal Judges: The Appointing Process," 51 *Minnesota Law Review* 185–218 (1966).

from above, or who desires to reflect local opinion by siding with one party to a case, has available a number of means for injecting his feelings into the proceedings. Not only can he state his views from the bench or incorporate them in a written opinion, he can also make them known by his acts. On his own volition he can deliberately delay his implementation of an objectionable order. He can entertain a motion to stay an objectionable order's implementation and find for the petitioner, knowing that an appeal will probably be taken against the ruling, thereby causing more delay. In any proceeding he can grant continuances. And to avoid a petition for injunctive relief that he does not desire to grant, he can refrain from setting a date for the hearing on the petition. He can also move other cases on the docket ahead of any proceedings he desires not to hear.

True, his tactics may result in his being made respondent in an action for relief brought by the aggrieved party. But although such actions against judges do happen, higher courts are extremely reluctant to grant remedies against an inferior judge that would control his discretion in the management of his court's business. Hence, district judges who are so disposed have ample opportunity to fulfill the "representational" role that Vines attributes to them.

Even though these modes for transmitting local viewpoints to the trial-court process are ever-present, certain factors do work for judicial integration and uniformity. Any well-disposed jurist, of course, will endeavor to identify and resist prejudicial influences. Moreover, working against localizing forces are such formal/informal factors as the District Court judge's desire for professional recognition and status and for the good opinion of his judicial peers and superiors. There are also the uniform rules of procedure, the possibility of appeals and reversal, the supervisory functions of judicial conferences, the lessons of bench books, the conserving principle of *stare decisis*, the force of legal training, the training effect of new judges seminars, and other agents of restraint.

How Much Local Influence?   At this point we ask, "To what, if any, extent should lower federal courts abide by local sentiments in their disposition of litigation? Is it permissible for them to do so at all?" On its face, the answer would seem to be emphatically in the negative, but the point cannot be denied that these courts, particularly the District Courts, do operate in a setting of local interests and sentiments, some of which, at least, may be powerful even though narrowly parochial. As is true of any court of law, the determinations of these courts must retain popular support and receive voluntary compliance if they are to function as effective instruments of social control. If they do not abide to some extent by local sentiment, it can be argued, they stand to lose all. A District Court may temporarily resist in the name of local sentiments the speedy imposition of national standards or of new statutory or constitutional doctrines. By so doing it may be able slowly to bring the people of its jurisdictional area around to acceptance of the new ways. By a gradual process of education in broader values, the essential link between local mores and a efficacious system of law can be preserved. But a District Court's dilatory tactics may sacrifice social objectives or the immediate realization of litigants' rights; and the lower courts may be compelled to give less than perfect adherence to what they know is the thrust of Supreme Court interpretation. To require the judiciary to tear up local institutions and destroy local values is more than lower-court judges are required by their office to do.

The question of local influence also involves the freedom of lower courts to control the course of litigation. They have long possessed considerable autonomy in internal administrative matters. The courts' long tradition of independence demonstrates the worth of administrative flexibility sufficient to permit adjustments to meet local conditions. Local procedures consistent with general rules are expressly permitted, so that considerable diversity is found in such things as the arrangement of calendars, printing of records, assignment of cases to judges, conduct of pre-trial hearings, and administration of charges to juries.

But suppose that in a doctrinal shift the Supreme Court should start adopting a liberal attitude toward particular types of cases by its granting of petitions for certiorari or by receiving appeals. That may encourage litigants to bring into the District Courts cases of the kind receiving favored treatment by the High Court. Suppose further that a trial judge is unsympathetic to the indicated doctrinal shift. May he use his administrative autonomy to oppose it in his court? Since control of his calendar rests with the trial judge, he may discriminate against the same class of cases that the Justices are favoring, all in the name of protecting the regular business of his court by reducing their effect upon its caseload. There is a valid, rather complex question (one that cannot be answered here) as to whether the Supreme Court should interfere too readily or extensively with a trial court's management of its docket. For such management is rightly based on the trial court's knowledge of its particular bench, the preparation of cases, the tactics of counsel, the special interests of the jurisdictional area served, and other related local factors. There can be no justification, however, for a trial or appellate court's using its local administrative autonomy to defeat reliance by local parties upon doctrinal interpretations with which lower judges disagree. At the same time, however, available studies of trial-court procedure indicate beyond doubt that these practices are indulged for judicially unacceptable reasons. The full extent and impact of that indulgence cannot be estimated with accuracy and perhaps will never be known.

Some Advantages of Localism. Localism in the District Courts has a positive side. The input of local values and influences mitigates the sterility of a dehumanized rule of law and is best achieved by a system of geographically dispersed courts. Decentralization serves the generally preferred proposition that impartiality and the absence of arbitrariness ought to attend the resolution of disputes. Decentralization does this by bringing abstract legalisms into direct contact with the realities of the facts out of which the cases originated, facts that will bear upon the efficacy of their resolution. The rule of law is always much colored by the impact of non-legal forces, and necessarily so, for while it orders society, it does so by meeting practical needs. To be effective, its rules must be accepted, and to be accepted they must be realistically adapted to the needs of the community.

Much local orientation of the law is regarded as good and is fostered by deliberate action of the High Court. Thus it has left to local application standards governing control of city streets, parks, and parades; it has substituted "local" standards for measuring obscenity[20] for the "national" standard of *Roth* v. *United States*;[21] it has accepted the principle that, inasmuch as anti-pollution measures must vary according to local conditions, states may go beyond national standards in enacting anti-pollution laws to protect their waterways and air. It has also allowed states to use a more flexible basis for drawing state legislative

20. *Miller* v. *California*, 413 U.S. 15 (1973).
21. 354 U.S. 476 (1957).

district lines than the rule of "absolute equality" insisted upon for congressional districting;[22] and, as a last example, it has permitted states "to legislate against what are found to be injurious practices in their internal commercial and business affairs"[23] according to their conceptions of local needs and interests.

Hence, justice through law is only in part a search for predictability, even-handedness, and fairness. It is also, and perhaps more importantly, a search for principles that are attuned to community acceptance and need but which at the same time are in tune with the requirements of constitutional principle. Parties who take their conflicts to District Courts for resolution must be *willing* to do so, not just as a move of expedience, but in the main because they are confident that the results they obtain will not be a rigid, undeviating adherence to precedent at the expense of relevant dissimilarities and adaptation to changed societal conditions. It is the District Courts primarily and the Courts of Appeals secondarily which provide particularized, updated, practical rules of law that the citizenry can live with. The District Courts are the principal providers of a system of judicial administration consistent enough to reassure the populace that the law will be acceptably regular, predictable, and certain in operation, as well as contemporary and practicable in substance.

The key to public confidence in legal justice lies in the particularization of law, but the key to the particularization of law lies in the exercise of judicial discretion. The District Courts do more than operate within a rigid framework of law (if "law" means statutes, administrative rules, and precedents), for the system of courts and the laws administered by them must be understood as embracing not only formalized rules, but also informal guidelines and largely undefined discretion, the latter being present in all phases of operation. In fact, the very essence of equity is the particularized application of known rules to various situations. Some individualization of justice and adaptation of formal rules of law to constantly changing social values

22. *Wesberry* v. *Sanders,* 376 U.S. 1 (1964), and *Kirkpatrick* v. *Preisler,* 394 U.S. 526 (1969).

23. *North Dakota Pharmacy Board* v. *Snyder's Stores,* 414 U.S. 156, 165 (1973), quoting and reaffirming *Lincoln Union* v. *Northwestern Co.,* 335 U.S. 525 (1949), and overruling *Liggett Co.* v. *Baldridge,* 278 U.S. 105 (1928).

is accomplished by legislative action, but judicial action provides a more important mechanism for maintaining adjustments between law and societal need. Indeed, the judiciary's great contribution to the law's efficacy is its constant injection of a dynamic element into the rules by which judges settle disputes.[24]

Because they are courts of first instance, the District Courts may be one of the points at which dissonance between legal rules and societal need is first registered. The evidence lies in the types and quantities of litigation brought to bar there. These courts can be expected to function as a bellwether indicating the degree of correlation between rules on the one hand and actual patterns of conduct and interests in society on the other. It is these courts' discretion, limited though it most certainly is, that enables them to identify dislocations between the black letter of laws and the regulation of social conflict. The products of judicial adjustment are embodied in precedents established.

The adaptation of general legal rules to the facts of concrete, specific cases can be thought of as equivalent to the District Courts' permitting entry of democratic influences into the decisional process. In their own way, the lower courts, especially the District Courts, because they are locally oriented, are more closely attuned to the public pulse than is their common superior. Hence, they, like their superior, represent an amalgam of political and legal influences and can only be properly understood in that character. Out of their processes comes not a sterile and legally homogenized judicial output, but one that is the product of a wide range of input variables, some legal, some political.

Courts in effect serve as forums in which spokesmen for parochial interests lacking general appeal and political clout can obtain a hearing for their pleas against the status quo. Thus courts fulfill a steadying function by affording to otherwise impotent and suppressed or ignored viewpoints a place in which they can be heard with some prospect of modifying the entrenched patterns of values, established procedures, or allocated resources.

Decisions of controversial cases by geographically dispersed District and appellate courts earn greater public notoriety within the judicial area of the court precisely because that

24. See E. H. Levi, *An Introduction to Legal Reasoning* (University of Chicago Press, 1948), pp. 1–5.

dispersion brings the issues out into the open at the local level and focuses attention upon them. Heightened public awareness and discussion of the merits of the controversy can be anticipated when the case is initiated, during its adjudication, when it is decided, when appeal is taken, and when appellate disposition is made. Depending upon the degree of public interest aroused, the local impact of litigation may range from zero to a high level of intensity. Regardless, the process always handles local situations locally.

However, these same local inputs attending lower-court litigation may reinforce existing conditions in a manner not to be taken lightly by the Supreme Court. Public sentiment—when it is generated by local disputes litigated in locally based courts, presided over by "hometown" judges, and determined by them or by locally resident juries—can prepare the ground in which the seeds of public policy or constitutional principle from the pods of Supreme Court decisions must be cultivated; the fruit they bear locally will depend upon the way they are received at the District Court level. Even though lower national courts are reversed, they may continue to affirm local interests and prejudices in their determinations of local issues and in their implementation of controversial public policies or constitutional principles. To the extent that they do this, they confirm and harden the entrenched parochial sense of what is right and tend to make the principles asserted by the High Court on reversal all the more disconcerting and unacceptable. The role of the lower court then becomes dysfunctional and the educative feature of Supreme Court pronouncements is impaired.

Factors Tending to Offset Localism. A number of factors tend to produce a national outlook in District Courts, thus offsetting local influence. All courts for the most part enforce national statutes and operate under common rules of civil and criminal procedure. All are jurisdictional coequals in the national judicial system and stand in a uniform position in their relationship to the Courts of Appeals and the Supreme Court. All are subject to the standardizing influence of the judicial council and conferences of the circuits and of the Judicial Conference of the United States. Judge's manuals and training seminars convey professional instruction and guidance and reinforce national orientation. Work handled by U.S. Attorneys' offices may be supervised by the Department of Justice, which often promulgates standards to guide the enforcement of national statutes before District Courts; and the Department may dispatch an attorney from Washington to handle any case it does not wish to leave to the resident U.S. Attorney. Formal and informal contacts between judicial personnel of a circuit serve as a reminder that all are members of the federal bench.[25]

THE IMPACT OF PERSONALITY

It is so easy to think of the federal constitutional courts as a monolithic judicial structure, all parts of which share common characteristics, purposes, values, and aspirations, that it becomes tempting to ignore the internal stresses and strains. Of course, all judges are involved with the administration of law and justice, but the interests represented, the functions performed, and the values served by the different types of courts are not the same. Many trial judges are justifiably proud of their positions on the bench, confident of their professional development, and self-assured of their knowledge of law and procedure, with the quite human result that they do not appreciate being reversed by higher authority. Even less do they like to be reprimanded, as occasionally happens, by a superior court. They normally obey instructions and conform to the decisions of higher courts; but protected by a judicial "distance" that separates them from their colleagues above, district judges sometimes let their real feelings show through in the form of criticism, now and then couched in surprisingly strong language. More rarely, a lower-court judge may become so provoked that he resorts to what in the orderly, restrained world of the judiciary amounts to insubordination, if not overt disobedience. On one such occasion District Court Judge Ashton H. Williams disqualified himself from presiding over an action brought to end racial segregation in public recreational facilities. Judge Williams destroyed any illusion that he was acting pursuant to the highest principles of judicial neutrality when he declared that the school desegregation decision was "unconstitutional" and said that "since as a Federal judge I have to follow that decision, I will disqualify myself because I have taken an oath to sustain the Constitution."[26]

Judge Williams was a moderate man compared to District

25. See R. A. Carp, "The Scope and Function of Intra-Circuit Judicial Communication," 6 *Law and Society Review* 407 (1972).
26. Reported in the *New York Times,* 8 September 1960, p. 27.

Court Judge William H. Atwell, who, having been called out of retirement at the age of 87, blatantly refused to accept or to enforce the *Brown* decision in his judicial district. He engaged in a protracted series of judicial duels with the Court of Appeals, Fifth Circuit, and although constantly on the losing end, refused to yield until at last the weight of his judicial obligations overcame his local prejudices and he declared: "It is difficult for me to approve such an order [of the Court of Appeals directing integration of the Texas public schools], but this is the law of the land and it is my duty to do what I am ordered to by a higher court."[27] And with openly acknowledged reluctance, District Judge Timmerman gave in to an order of the Fourth Circuit Court of Appeals directing him to initiate integration of the municipal airport facilities of Greenville, South Carolina. He said:

> That holding has the appearance of groping after a plausible excuse for according preferential treatment to some class. However, appellate rulings are nevertheless binding and must be followed.[28]

These, however, are unusual instances. All arose out of a subject about which there was intense sectional feeling deeply held and long entrenched; and all arose out of circumstances ideally suited to resistance. Remember that when the Supreme Court directed the District Courts to implement *Brown* v. *Board of Education*[29] it left them maximum discretion to accommodate local conditions, but subject to the assumption that local acceptance and judicial supervision would rest upon the good faith of all concerned.

THE SOCIALIZATION OF JUDGES

The novice District Court judge finds himself immediately in a sink-or-swim situation. Even those who have had prior service on a state-court bench are apt to feel apprehensive. For both they and their wholly inexperienced fellows are required almost immediately to take up their responsibilities without instruction in their duties. The opportunity for a judge to receive

---

27. Reported in 2 *Race Relations Law Reporter* 985 (1957), at p. 986.
28. *Henry* v. *Greenville Airport Commission*, 191 F. Supp. 146 (1960).
29. 347 U.S. 483 (1954) and 349 U.S. 294 (1955).

some instruction at a Seminar for New Judges at the National Judicial Institute may come in the initial days or weeks of his service, but more likely it will not come for several months or a year. Judges of a civil-law system, on the other hand, undergo extensive preparation and examination to qualify for initial appointment to a minor-court bench, and only after they have served on minor courts do they succeed to more prestigious positions. In contrast, the American national process of judicial selection places minimal emphasis on legal training, stressing political "availability" instead. Thus the neophyte District Court judge is thrown for his judicial education upon such resources as he can muster for himself and as may be thoughtfully extended to him by colleagues. How well he handles the substantive and procedural aspects of his tribunal's business during his breaking-in period will have a direct effect upon his relations with higher courts and contribute to or detract from his professional standing, perhaps for some time to come.

The assistance that new district judges get from their colleagues comes primarily from within their own courts and almost exclusively from district judges within the circuit.[30] This assistance is a major factor in perpetuating the impact of local influences upon the national trial courts. Because jurisdictional districts are small, on most ordinary issues there will rarely be sharp differences of influence and response between judges in the same district, particularly if the region has homogeneous values, institutions, and traditions. Nevertheless, there is much evidence that the theoretical uniformity of national law is diminished and localized by the force of parochial considerations. District judges bring some of these factors with them as personal orientations at the time of their appointment; but still more impinge on them thereafter. This continuous local input comes from court officers like clerks (who probably come from their judge's own in-state law school), probation officers (whose pre-sentence reports are largely of a sociological nature), state judges (with whom the district judge may have personal or other contacts), local civic leaders, and local attorneys. Local input also comes through the way legal issues are presented in litigation brought before the court, and through the local press.

30. See Carp and Wheeler, "Sink or Swim: The Socialization of a Federal District Judge," 21 *Journal of Public Law* 359 (1959), at p. 374, on which this section is based.

Although the Judicial Conference of the Circuit[31] is an agent of judicial socialization, it cannot eliminate the effects of inexperience from the operation and intercourt relationships of the circuit. The burden of inexperience is multidimensional. The new district judge may have to learn much of the substantive content of admiralty, bankruptcy, patent and copyright, labor, taxation, antitrust, criminal, and other important areas of national law that he has not contended with in his preappointment career. At the same time, he must learn the rules and perfect the procedures of conducting an arraignment, charging a jury, conducting a *voir dire*, sentencing convicted persons, and carrying on pre-trial hearings to maximum benefit. He must adjust to the isolation of his new position, and to the responsibility it imposes on him. He must get used to new patterns of behavior and standards appropriate to his new status, to the alteration of prior social and professional relationships, and to the reorientation of professional outlook demanded by his new role as a dispassionate, neutral third party. He must learn to manage the docket with maximum efficiency, utilize the skills of his court's supporting personnel, and economize his own time and energy for optimum use.

A judge who is still learning his craft affects relations between his court and others within the structure. For example, a neophyte's errors of procedure and law may increase the number of appeals taken to higher levels. His failure to make maximum use of pre-trial proceedings and his inability to make informed, speedy rulings or in other ways to maintain a firm control of the caseload in his courtroom may cause his docket to grow so long that the temporary help of a colleague may be needed to clear up the backlog.

Thus in such ways will an individual judge and his court bear the burden of his inexperience; so also may the judicial system as a whole. The consequences of inexperience, however, depend on myriad imponderables and are the product of many individual situations; for this reason they are not subject to precise measurement or evaluation.

31. This conference is composed of the district and appeals judges of the circuit. It meets annually and is presided over by the chief judge of the circuit.

CHAPTER 5

The Courts of Appeals

Courts of Appeals are perhaps the least-noticed of the regular constitutional courts. Their activities are not dramatic. Most proceedings before them are conducted in staid fashion before almost empty courtrooms, and they normally receive little notice by the press. Appellate judges have close, continuous contact only with their clerks, with appellate counsel, and with one another, and even the latter may not be very close. The business that comes to the appellate courts has for the most part already been put through an adjudicative process by a court or administrative agency.

Since 1968, standard rules of procedure have tended to make the operation of Courts of Appeals more uniform, but local differences are still found. So, too, are diverse internal arrangements for reaching decisions, holding conferences, preparing opinions, and making results known. Some appellate courts have larger caseloads, handle cases more expeditiously, and reach decisions with a higher degree of unanimity than do others.[1]

Internal divisions of judges into discernible voting blocs have been found to be a common feature of their decision-making

1. See S. Goldman, "Conflict and Consensus in the United States Courts of Appeals," *Wisconsin Law Review* 461–482 (1968).

processes.[2] Blocs formed along "liberal" and "conservative" lines have been correlated to patterns of decision-making. Bloc alignments induce internal compromise, reflect personal values of judges, and reduce unanimity in decisions reached.

SOURCES AND TYPES OF CASES

A brief look at certain features of the U.S. Courts of Appeals may make clearer their position in the national court structure and help in understanding their relationship to the Supreme Court. Almost all of their business is derived from the District Courts,[3] but unlike the Supreme Court they have no ability to screen the number and types of cases or the issues of law they will accept to review. Their judges' most significant opportunity for the exercise of independence comes at the time of decision.

At first impression, one might conclude that all business coming up to the eleven Courts of Appeals is important and of approximately equal significance, but in fact a wide variety of cases, many of which are devoid of legal merit or public significance, fall within their purview. Much appellate litigation is either trivial or *pro forma* and in either instance is easily disposed of. Such appeals may be taken because of the pressure of community sentiment, or because of the persistence of a well-heeled and determined litigant. Appellants in these cases have virtually no chance of prevailing above, but appeal provides an excellent means by which to release tensions felt by communities, parties, or judges through giving them a chance to vent their views.

Use of courts by the government to gain its ends and use of

2. S. Goldman, "Voting Behavior on the United States Courts of Appeals, 1961–1964," 60 *American Political Science Review* 374–383 (1966); also L. S. Loeb, "Judicial Blocs and Judicial Values in Civil Liberties Cases Decided by the Supreme Court and the United States Court of Appeals for the District of Columbia Circuit," 14 *American University Law Review* 149 (1965).

3. During fiscal 1973 a total of 141,715 cases were disposed of by the District Courts, of which 98,259 were civil and 43,456 were criminal. From *Annual Report of the Director*, 1973, table 13, p. 115. During the same period, 15,629 appeals were filed, of which 13,329 came up from District Courts. The remainder consisted of 1,616 administrative, 338 bankruptcy, and 346 original proceedings (under jurisdiction by writs of mandamus and, less frequently, of prohibition). Ibid., table B–1.

courts by aggrieved parties to review determinations by government agencies account for approximately 28 percent of the appellate tribunals' business. Such actions seldom raise far-reaching issues of public policy or provide serious setbacks to the administrative processes of government, though the review of government agency determinations does more frequently modify administrative procedures or decisions.

The remainder of the appellate courts' business has been divided by Richardson and Vines into "consensual" and "non-consensual" appeals. "Consensual" appeals are those taken up from a District Court in spite of general agreement among courts and authorities as to how the issue ought to be disposed of; "non-consensual" appeals, by contrast, are appeals raising for the first time broad, controversial public-policy questions about which no established position has been identified in precedent.[4]

More important than the percentage of total District Court "dispositions" taken up to the Courts of Appeals is the ratio of cases appealed to the number *decided* in the District Courts. The District Courts in fiscal 1973 terminated 19,467 *trials* (10,896 civil and 8,571 criminal). Of these, an impressive number of 13,329 (8,876 civil and 4,453 criminal) cases were appealed. Hence 81 percent of civil trials and 52 percent of criminal trials produced appeals.[5]

Some delay is a normal feature of the appellate process, but the Courts of Appeals manage to dispose of their caseloads with reasonable expedition by such measures as extensive use of three-judge panels sitting concurrently at different places within a circuit, culling the dockets, combining cases raising like questions on similar facts, utilizing the most expeditious procedures, achieving resolution of issues without going through full hearing, benefiting from occasional withdrawals of suits by litigants, and rejecting suits that fail to meet technical requirements. Out of the culling and screening emerge the items of business raising meritorious questions—and sometimes, but not as often as popular impression would have it, they are questions of major public law or policy content. Tables 7 and 8 set forth the median time intervals for cases terminated after hearing or submission.

4. R. J. Richardson and K. Vines, *The Politics of Federal Courts* (Little, Brown, 1970), pp. 118–119.

5. Data taken from *Annual Report of the Director*, 1973, table D–4, p. 402, and table C–4, p. 358.

TABLE 7

U.S. COURTS OF APPEALS,
MEDIAN TIME INTERVALS IN CRIMINAL CASES
TERMINATED AFTER HEARING OR SUBMISSION,
FISCAL YEAR ENDED JUNE 30, 1973

Circuit	From filing of complete record to final disposition		From filing of complete record to filing last brief		From filing last brief to hearing or submission		From hearing or submission to final disposition	
	Cases	Interval (months)	Cases	Interval (months)	Cases	Interval (months)	Cases	Interval (months)
Total	3,104	5.5	3,014	2.5	3,014	1.3	3,104	1.0
District of Columbia	282	10.2	278	5.2	278	3.3	282	.7
First	60	6.4	58	4.4	58	.4	60	1.3
Second	434	3.8	424	2.6	424	.2	434	.4
Third	220	6.1	209	2.9	209	2.1	220	.6
Fourth	238	5.7	209	2.8	209	1.1	238	1.2
Fifth	484	4.3	469	2.0	469	1.4	484	.5
Sixth	205	6.7	205	2.9	205	2.2	205	.6
Seventh	207	9.6	205	5.0	205	1.8	207	2.3
Eighth	162	4.5	150	2.2	150	1.1	162	1.1
Ninth	646	4.9	653	2.1	653	1.3	646	1.0
Tenth	166	5.8	154	2.8	154	1.3	166	1.2

SOURCE: *Annual Report of the Director*, 1973, Table B–4b, p. 311.

THE STYLE OF APPELLATE PROCEEDINGS

Proceedings in U.S. appellate courts vary considerably from court to court, and the impact of individual judicial personalities is never absent. However, there are certain features in common. Appellate-court proceedings differ markedly from those of the trial courts. Whereas trial judges are almost passive participants, appellate-court judges have the opportunity to be as active as they desire. Ordinarily they interrogate counsel freely on his points and authorities as he advances them in oral presentation or by brief. Appellate judges share no responsibility or lime-light with a jury because none is ever used in their court. Most cases are decided on their merits after hearing or submission, since those brought up on appeal are rarely withdrawn from the decisional process; and cases terminated are dealt with in open court inasmuch as none are disposed of by pre-trial proceedings or proceedings in chambers.

Appellate courts are typically concerned with questions of law and public policy, as contrasted with issues of fact, which command the attention of trial courts. Hence, the most common

TABLE 8

U.S. COURTS OF APPEALS,
MEDIAN TIME INTERVALS IN CIVIL AND CRIMINAL CASES
TERMINATED AFTER HEARING OR SUBMISSION,
FISCAL YEAR ENDED JUNE 30, 1973

Circuit	From filing notice of appeal in lower court to filing of complete record in appellate court				From docketing in lower court to final disposition in appellate court			
	Civil		Criminal		Civil		Criminal	
	Cases	Interval (months)	Cases	Interval (months)	Cases	Interval (months)	Cases	Interval (months)
Total	5,728	1.3	3,104	1.7	5,728	19.0	3,101	15.8
District of Columbia	237	1.2	282	1.8	237	26.1	282	22.5
First	138	.4	60	.2	138	15.4	60	17.2
Second	420	1.2	434	1.3	420	17.3	434	15.8
Third	415	1.3	220	1.3	415	24.1	220	19.9
Fourth	889	.9	238	1.4	889	14.0	238	13.3
Fifth	1,445	1.3	484	1.5	1,445	18.6	484	13.6
Sixth	459	1.3	205	2.7	459	18.3	205	16.5
Seventh	354	1.3	207	2.3	354	21.8	207	22.3
Eighth	327	2.5	162	2.5	327	19.7	162	13.2
Ninth	536	2.0	646	2.3	536	26.4	646	13.5
Tenth	508	1.4	166	2.3	508	14.9	166	12.8

SOURCE: *Annual Report of the Director*, 1973, Table B–5, p. 311.

activity before an appellate tribunal is argument, in which each counsel orally states his position, clarifies points, and responds to questions from the bench. Appellate briefs and oral presentations are the modes by which precedents, principles, and ideas are conveyed to the judges. In contrast, a trial is a means enabling parties to present evidence, hear the evidence of the other party, and have the opportunity to meet that evidence by argument, presentation and cross-examination; and the entire trial process culminates in a decision on the record.

Proceedings in the appellate courts are, therefore, based on the record made in the trial court below and on comprehensive briefs setting out the appellate arguments of counsel and their supporting legal authorities. Briefs are filed before a hearing date is set. The case proceeds on the issues which have been developed below and made the focus of the appeal, as set out in the briefs and amplified by oral presentation before the judges. Prior to argument, the three judges who have been selected to hear the case normally research the legal citations and study the briefs. The procedure of hearing and decision is somewhat like that of the Supreme Court. The presiding judges almost never announce their decision immediately after argument ends, even though it is possible for them to confer and reach a decision without leaving the bench. By overwhelmingly common practice, cases are discussed, voted upon, and decided in conference. The writing of the opinion is then assigned, drafts are circulated when ready, and then later the decision is announced concurrently with the opinion being made known in final form. Written opinions support the decisions and state the reasoning of the judges. Unanimity, of course, is not required: dissents are frequent. At least two judges sign the court's opinion, but those who sign—thereby indicating acceptance of its content —are not necessarily equal coauthors of the opinion.

ENDS SERVED BY THE COURTS OF APPEALS

The Courts of Appeals perform several functions that in part control relations between themselves and the District Courts. By correcting errors of District Court judges, they provide an opportunity for the review of trial-court findings to assure *justice to the parties* in matters of law and procedure. For, like District Courts, they are not public-law tribunals but exist primarily to serve the interests of litigants.

Because the circuits are large and contain an average of nine District Courts, the possibility is constantly present that two trial courts in a circuit will decide essentially the same question in different ways. If such divergence were to remain unresolved, the uniformity of national law would suffer and might even disappear, and the difficulties of lawyers attempting to ascertain its rules would be compounded. The resolution of legal controversies in federal courts would become a variable of geographic location, and the clamor of competing interests caught up in litigious situations and seeking recognition through judicial acceptance would approach the bedlam of directionless minds in an asylum. The Court of Appeals, then, is a first step (and, for a vast preponderance of cases, a last step) in the process by which uniformity is instilled into national law. The circuit judges sit in judgment of the work of the trial judges in this as in other respects, even though some disagreement, dissatisfaction, or suspicion may thereby be generated below.

Great misunderstanding, however, surrounds just how great the therapeutic effect of appeal or the threat of appeal is upon the relationships of District with appellate courts and judges. Although all judges of the federal judicial system share a consciousness of what has been referred to as the "cult of the robe," those who sit on the trial courts may (and in fact sometimes do) feel a sense of rivalry toward, rather than kinship with, their judicial superiors. The federal trial judge who knows a sense of professional pride, who aspires to higher appointment, who desires to stand well in the estimation of his colleagues (superiors as well as those of equal rank)—the trial judge who does not wish to incur the criticism of the legal profession in its many parts, who desires, in other words, to be regarded as a "good judge" by professional critics—does not want to be reversed on the merits or because he committed a procedural error during his conduct of a trial.

Not all trial judges respond positively to these considerations, however; some are unconscious of their self-disciplining influence. And although there is some evidence that particular lower-court judges in time come to be held by courts above in particularly high esteem, there is an almost total absence of data to show that being overruled does in fact subject a judge to the low opinion of his fellow jurists. Moreover, there is little evidence that lower-court judges on a multi-judge bench covertly and informally rate each other's performance. Nevertheless, there are enough published evaluations of their colleagues by various members of the Supreme Court to reveal that the practice is freely indulged in on that tribunal; and, if there, why not on the courts below? It is, in fact, a psychological inevitability that the members of any collegial body will rate their associates.

Knowledge by a judge that his decisions and rulings can be appealed, that findings of prejudicial error carry some imputation of incompetence, and that his professional reputation and good standing may ride on any decision he reaches can only benefit the competent, impartial administration of justice to litigants. It is probably correct to say that the appellate function of the intermediate tribunals eliminates from the administration of federal justice the worst instances of error committed by district judges, but only when the aggrieved party is able and willing to seek rectification above.

The Courts of Appeals neutralize much of the particularism and localism that are sometimes excessively reflected by District judges, in much the same way that the Supreme Court of the United States eliminates conflicts of interpretation created by the diverse decisions of appellate judges. As was noted above, each judicial circuit, except for that of the District of Columbia, is composed of several states, and thus each circuit tends to reflect a distinctly regional character. For example, the First Circuit, embracing the states of Maine, New Hampshire, Massachusetts, and Rhode Island and the Territory of Puerto Rico, has a distinct New England flavor; and that of the Fifth Circuit, consisting in major part of Alabama, Florida, Georgia, Louisiana, Mississippi, and Texas, has a deep-South complexion. Judges need not live within the circuits at the time of their appointment, but most do; those who do not must take up residence at some place within their jurisdictions after ascending the bench. Sectional coloration of the appellate courts is mitigated by the fact that since the areas are usually large, or, if small, tend to contain a large population with heterogeneous interests, a variety of viewpoints is to be found within each circuit and is reflected by its judges.

Compared to the sometime parochialism of District Court judges, Courts of Appeals judges show a distinctly panoramic outlook. Local politics probably counts for less in Circuit Court appointments than it does in District Court appointments. A careful selection of judges from states within the circuit having dissimilar interests, values, and cultural orientations can dilute parochial sentiment within the Circuit bench. Localism can also be countered by making temporary assignments of one or more judges to serve on a tribunal when a modification of outlook on matters of public policy or legal principle is desired, though numerous considerations of propriety and practical difficulties may make such a step unwise. On the other hand, the composition of three-judge panels can also be arranged so as to present a more nearly uniform front.

Failure by the Supreme Court to provide guidance for lower courts can have a most disruptive effect upon intercourt relationships. Such failure to provide adequate guidance has nowhere generated greater uncertainty or been more productive of litigation than in the matter of desegregation through court-ordered busing of school children. With much implication of studied purpose, the Supreme Court until 1974[6] failed to rule

6. *Milliken* v. *Bradley*, 418 U.S. 717 (1974). The history of this subject after *Swann* v. *Charlotte-Mecklenburg Board of Education*, 402 U.S. 1 (1971), is explored in R. I. Richter, "School Desegregation after Swann: A Theory of Government Responsibility," 39 *University of Chicago Law Review* 421 (Winter 1972).

on *de facto* segregation and to provide definitive rulings or guidelines on compulsory busing and other practical problems of desegregation. Case-by-case determinations by lower courts in the almost complete absence of standards from above produced much lay and official public confusion concerning all aspects of the issue and generated numerous real and apparent contradictions among their decisions.

Courts of Appeals, however, can have a steadying effect on official and public reaction to a contentious decision by a District Court that grows out of the vacuum left by the Supreme Court's silence. Coming after a long period of mounting emotional tension and divided public feeling, District Court decisions on busing triggered a movement pressing for hasty, extremist, and perhaps ill-advised legislative action. Such pressure was alleviated by appellate action. Reversal by the Court of Appeals, Fourth Circuit, of the decision of District Court Judge Robert H. Merhige in the Richmond, Virgina, school busing case provided such welcome relief. It also helped to clarify the urgent need for a High Court ruling on the constitutionality of *de facto* segregation in public education, and also for the setting of standards to guide public officials and lower courts confronted by legal actions growing out of the explosive issue of school consolidation and busing of children. The Circuit Court action in this instance provided time for additional deliberation, allowed tempers to cool, and advanced the case for putting some rational restraints on mass busing.

The appellate decision had several political results. Reversal abated public concern over the innovating decisions of one-judge District Courts across the nation. First, District judges were told that busing was *an* acceptable solution for redressing racial imbalance only if "invidious state action" could be shown, and that absent such a showing, they lacked authority to order wholesale reorganization of the school systems. Second, the decision calmed taxpayer and official concern over the need to make great expenditures for school buses for court-ordered busing. Third, by staying progress toward large-scale busing and by holding out the prospect of Supreme Court review of the entire issue, it apparently also contributed to passage by the House of Representatives of the socially important Aid to Elementary and Secondary Education bill. Coming when the House was deeply divided by dissension over anti-busing amendments to the bill, the message of relief from the Fourth Circuit stimulated the making of compromises that were generally hailed as the best moderate accommodations possible.

The above chain of events illustrates how appellate-court consequences may extend far beyond the interests of the parties to a case. Here, appellate intermediation permitted delay in complying with the District Court's order until many questions of invalidity could be resolved. The episode shows the vast financial, psychological, and political impact that decisions can have upon local authorities, taxpayers, community structure, parents, and school children. It demonstrates how inferior courts by a series of geographically separated rulings related to a common social problem can enter the arena of policy-making involving a highly emotional subject. And it shows how the lower courts can lead higher courts in breaking new legal ground, perhaps eventually forcing the higher courts to enter a policy area out of which they might wish to stay. It reveals how a Court of Appeals can intercede to cut off policy innovation by District Courts, relieve pressure on public officials, provide cooling-off time for heated tempers, and allow the Supreme Court to intervene.

The Courts of Appeals protect the Supreme Court from the flood of meritless appeals that might otherwise engulf it, and thus they leave it free to perform its historic role in the constitutional system.[7] The intermediate appellate tribunals provide the opportunity for one appeal which is guaranteed by statute to every litigant in a national court who can and will use it. By being available to that end, they exert some chastening influence upon trial-court judges, occasionally redressing serious errors below and improving the quality of justice administered in the trial courts. Reconciling decisional differences in like cases and ensuring procedural regularity, they homogenize law and procedure within the circuit. They decentralize the availability of appellate review, thereby making it more accessible, less costly, and more convenient for litigants, with the result that public ability and willingness to utilize the working courts of the constitutional structure is enhanced.

7. Analysis of appellate-court decision-making can be found in Kenneth Vines, "The Role of the Circuit Courts of Appeal in the Federal Judicial Process: A Case Study," 7 *Midwest Journal of Political Science* 305–319 (1963).

To a large extent, formal rules of jurisdiction and procedure control what the Courts of Appeals can do with the cases brought to them as well as what, if anything, can be done next with them. Formal rules also constrain appellate-court procedures and other aspects of their discretion. Within the limiting effect of such rules, however, Courts of Appeals filter the cases brought up from the District Courts, picking out the few that present potentially important questions raising significant policy issues from among the many that do not. Although they are compelled to operate *on* the record from below—the facts, the issues raised, and the rules and precedents presented therein— they seemingly have ample scope within the gaps and vagaries of law and precedent and behind the shield of procedural and substantive error alleged below to make far-reaching and innovative reshaping of issues. The appellate tribunals can and do take cases that were routine below, find in them previously sublimated or novel features not brought out below, and transform them into actions of great political consequence.

Accordingly, therefore, the role of Courts of Appeals vis-a-vis the District Courts, in one direction, and the Supreme Court, in the other, is more than acting to screen litigation or stem its flow. Appellate courts also transmute issues, redirecting the force of facts so that the case taken on appeal is not the same litigation originally tried and decided below. Thus appellate courts make it possible to introduce new policy issues at an intermediate point in the judicial hierarchy. Even if the litigation is not carried beyond the Courts of Appeals, the net effect is that issues tried below are transformed and decided in their metamorphosed form, without their having been challenged before or decided by the High Court. Because the transformations brought about at the appellate level can be dramatic and novel, those courts in effect generate and can finally resolve weighty policy questions. Their significance in the judicial structure, therefore, is much greater than their intermediate position suggests.[8]

---

8. Richardson and Vines, "Review, Dissent and the Appellate Process: A Political Interpretation," 29 *Journal of Politics* 597 (1967), at p. 601; also Sheldon Goldman and Thomas Jahnige, *The Federal Courts As a Political System* (Harper & Row, 1971), p. 193.

DECISION-MAKING BY COURTS OF APPEALS

Like those of the High Court, decisions of Courts of Appeals are always reached by collegial groups. However, while the Supreme Court always sits *en banc*, intermediate appellate tribunals for the most part employ panels of only three judges.

Three-Judge Panels. For each case to be heard, a separate panel is created. Unanimity among the judges of a panel is common. Panels created at random might not be expected to produce unanimity of view on controversial policy issues with a high degree of consistency; yet up to 90 percent of panel decisions have been found to be unanimous. The probability that panels will reach a common stand on difficult issues is increased first by their collegial character and second by the high visibility of dissent. Nevertheless, a panel can be constructed so as to cause a predetermined outcome, and the filling of a vacancy caused by the illness or death of a member can shift the decisional balance even though every effort is made to select the replacement by a wholly objective procedure.

Eight of the eleven circuit tribunals have assigned to them a sufficiently large number of judges to permit the selection of at least one judge from each state comprising the circuit, so that a panel will normally include at least two judges from states other than that in which the case arose. How much real value this circumstance has for litigants and for the impartial administration of justice is uncertain and needs further research. It is probably slight, and also least effective when most needed—whenever, that is, a strongly felt regional interest is threatened by the allegations of a party. Moreover, a decision rendered by part of a court is somehow robbed of some of the prestige and intangible respect it would command if it were the product of full-court action (although in law it is, of course, no less authoritative and binding).

In the context of a three-judge panel, the authority of dissent as a force for influencing the course of future decisions is greatly reduced. The dissenter can never have support on a dissent; he simply registers his disagreement against his other two colleagues with whom he has been temporarily thrown together to make up a panel. He can be identified as a member of a policy-oriented group, if at all, only after persistent disaffection has clearly set him apart. Because the court as a whole rarely determines a sufficient number of similar policy-oriented cases to establish a clear intracourt division, each dissenter tends to stand, and be viewed as standing, alone. The futility of dissent may promote unanimity of judgment within panels.[9]

Attorneys and trial-court judges complain about the use of panels, for to some extent it makes the resolution of litigation dependent upon an attorney's luck in the drawing of his judges. It gives personality factors and the ideological variations that are to be found among most groups of appellate-court judges a magnified importance in the decision-making process. It vests in three judges authority to decide issues in the name of the full court, ignoring the ever-present possibility that a different decision might be reached if all members of the bench participated in the outcome. The selection process, it has been asserted, in many instances is little more than a lottery which turns review by a Court of Appeals into a game of chance, and what is one party's bad fortune may very well be the good luck of the other.[10] The use of three-judge panels, in other words, injects a fortuitous element into the decisional process of intermediate appellate courts, one that its critics argue should play no part in the administration of legal justice.

The possibility that the composition of three-judge panels can be manipulated has been asserted. In fact, the mode of their selection in one court has drawn a strong protest from an intermediate appellate judge.[11] Judge Ben F. Cameron of the Fifth Circuit Court of Appeals surveyed twenty-nine civil rights cases decided by his court during a two-year period prior to June 26, 1963. Twenty-five of them he found to have been decided by panels with a majority of pro-civil-rights judges, although that bloc of judges numbered only four, a minority of the full bench. The four were Chief Judge Elbert F. Tuttle, and Judges Richard T. Rives, John Minor Wisdom, and John R. Brown, who stood together with noticeable consistency in civil-rights cases coming to their tribunal. By local practice the Chief Judge designated the personnel of panels. In only four instances, then, did this group fail to dominate the review of these important cases, according to Judge Cameron's findings. They sat, *in toto*, sixty-

9. S. Goldman, "Conflict and Consensus in the United States Courts of Appeals," *Wisconsin Law Review* 461 (1968), at p. 481.

10. Wiener, "Federal Regional Courts: A Solution for the Certiorari Dilemma," 44 *ABA Journal* 1169 (1963), at p. 1170.

11. Judge Cameron's findings can be found in his dissenting opinion of *Armstrong* v. *Board* reported in 323 F. 2d 333 (1963), at p. 358.

three times whereas the remaining five members of the court sat only fourteen times. The substance of Judge Cameron's indictment was that the Chief Judge had stacked the panels of civil-rights cases appealed to his court from the federal District Courts of the circuit so that they would be decided favorably to the black claimant.

Whether or not Judge Cameron's allegations were justified, the influence of a Chief Judge over composition of the panels (and therefore over their tendency to resolve issues having ideological overtones) can be significant. It is a source of much potential influence, and perhaps control, for him. If he is judicially out of step with his court or circuit, he may use discretion to create panels that produce desired outcomes; and should he feel the need of support he may activate a senior judge having the appropriate views. Such a use of panels would magnify ideological differences identifying blocs of judges within a tribunal, and thereby increase the probability of rigid internal divisions, stimulate intracourt conflict, and obstruct compromise.

In sum, what the Supreme Court reviews as an appellate-court product is clearly that more by courtesy than by fact. Except when a Court of Appeals sits *en banc*,[12] "its" decision is only that of a portion of the tribunal's membership and may or may not accurately mirror the decisional product of the bench as a whole.

En Banc Proceedings. The use of panels enables an appellate court to dispose of a greater number of cases than would be possible if each case had to be heard and decided by a full court, but it also creates the possibility that conflicting decisions will be rendered by different panels of the same court in like cases and that the Supreme Court will be induced thereby to intervene in order to restore uniformity. *En banc* procedure has been devised as a curb on the operation of three-judge panels and to guard against the shortcomings of their use. It is infrequently used because it is reserved for exceptionally important questions and to harmonize divergent panel decisions; moreover, *en banc* hearing "is not favored and ordinarily will not be ordered except" for those reasons.[13]

Practice varies in detail from court to court, but the usual mode of protection is to provide for a full-court hearing before

12. The full court, rather than panels or divisions, sits to hear a case.
13. See Rules for Appellate Procedure, 28 U.S.C., Appendix, Rule 35(a).

the decision of a three-judge panel becomes final. To that end, the Circuit Courts are authorized by statute to sit *en banc*. That some such proceeding be sanctioned is especially important inasmuch as many determinations of the panels stand unreviewed; and without the possibility of full-court review the uncertainties of contrary results arrived at by different panels in seemingly indistinguishable cases would too often be left unresolved. Since such a consequence would be intolerable in a judicial system based on the principle of *stare decisis*, the full task of resolution would have had to be passed on to the Supreme Court, thereby increasing the burden on its operation.

Each Court of Appeals is competent to regulate the specific manner by which it will provide a full-court hearing.[14] Some courts tend to be very reluctant to authorize an *en banc* hearing; others are more liberal. A request for an *en banc* hearing may be originated by either a member of the panel concerned with the case or by a non-panel member of the court. Litigants usually suggest the suitability of a case for an *en banc* hearing, but neither a panel nor a full court is bound to act on a litigant's proposal. In all courts the procedure may be invoked before a panel makes its findings known; in most it is employed after the panel's decision has been revealed. In some courts a majority of active members must support a request for an *en banc* hearing; for others the support of a lesser number is sufficient.

In spite of the apparent ease with which a full-court hearing may be had, *en banc* procedure is seldom used. Examination of Table 9 reveals that in fiscal 1973 use was more evenly distributed among the appellate courts than in 1972, but in both 1972 and 1973 *en banc* procedure was employed for only about .035 percent of the hearings held. The Court of Appeals, First Circuit, has abstained entirely from using the procedure for the last three years.[15]

Clearly, the purpose of the rehearing process by a full court is not only to enable it to exercise a general supervisory power over the work of its own panels of judges, but also to provide a means for eliminating conflict between decisions of panels. The relation of the full court to a panel is not that of a superior

14. Use of *en banc* procedure has been sanctioned by the Supreme Court in *Textile Mills Corporation* v. *Commissioner*, 314 U.S. 326 (1941).

15. For a more complete analysis of *en banc* procedure see J. L. Labovitz, "En Banc Procedure in the Federal Courts of Appeals," 111 *University of Pennsylvania Law Review* 220 (1962), at p. 224.

TABLE 9

U.S. COURTS OF APPEALS,
HEARINGS HELD,
FISCAL YEARS 1971, 1972, AND 1973

Circuit	Fiscal year 1971			Fiscal year 1972			Fiscal year 1973		
	Total	En banc	By panels of the court	Total	En banc	By panels of the court	Total	En banc	By panels of the court
Total	5,816	51	5,765	5,748	20	5,728	6,555	23	6,532
District of Columbia	417	9	408	367	6	361	381	3	378
First	155	—	155	175	—	175	190	—	190
Second	774	3	771	735	—	735	883	—	883
Third	419	14	405	422	—	422	361	2	359
Fourth	331	9	322	346	5	341	352	1	351
Fifth	848	11	837	702	9	693	778	4	774
Sixth	624	—	624	705	—	705	733	2	731
Seventh	482	2	480	517	—	517	667	3	664
Eighth	405	3	402	441	—	441	500	5	495
Ninth	988	—	988	912	—	912	1,266	1	1,265
Tenth	373	—	373	426	—	426	444	2	442

SOURCE: *Annual Report of the Director*, 1972, p. 100; and ibid., 1973, p. 106.

tribunal to an inferior one. The decision of a panel is not in any sense appealed to a full court; the full court does not review what the panel has done nor does it "remand" the case if *en banc* procedure is authorized. But the procedure seems to have transferred the force of dissent from the panel to the full court, for decisions of *en banc* cases produce much intracourt dispute.[16]

THE VARIABLE STANDING OF APPELLATE COURTS

The Courts of Appeals possess varying importance in the eyes of the Supreme Court and probably also in the eyes of one another. But the constantly changing status of their personnel and the variable consequences of their business for the public make relative and temporary any superiority that might be enjoyed by one of them over its peers. A random, fortuitous assemblage of superb judicial ability may, however, distinguish one appellate court from its sister tribunals. So it was when

16. A. L. Alexander, "En Banc Hearings in the Federal Courts of Appeals: Accommodating Institutional Responsibilities," 40 *New York University Law Review* 583 (1965).

Augustus and Learned Hand sat with Jerome Frank as judges of the Court of Appeals, Second Circuit. That court was then regarded by many lawyers and other judges as the second-ranking tribunal in the nation, surpassed only by the Supreme Court. Some gave it first place. But those judges are now all dead, and the Second Circuit, although still important because of its position in relation to the economic, commercial, and financial heart of America, does not today possess the prestige it formerly enjoyed.

The nature of judicial business also affects the significance of a Court of Appeals and the character of its relations with the Supreme Court. When the major problems of public policy and law centered on corporations, business, and property, the Second Circuit tribunal enjoyed an importance that has abated somewhat because the important questions of older days have been answered and newer ones, focused upon other circuits, have arisen to command national attention. The rise of bureaucratic government has done much to focus attention on the Court of Appeals for the District of Columbia, for that tribunal is the statutory recipient of appeals from many of the most active regulatory and administrative agencies, and it has jurisdiction over national executive officers against whom legal process may be sought. Similarly, the rise of civil-liberties litigation involving racial discrimination has been concentrated in the deep South, so that the Court of Appeals, Fifth Circuit, took on an importance in the 1960's which it previously did not possess and which in the 1970's began to recede.

During the ascendancy of the Court of Appeals, Second Circuit, it was evident that the Supreme Court accepted its findings and the rationale of its opinions with less reluctance and less close scrutiny than it did those of courts not so favored. A display of deference by a Justice is, of course, a purely individual and personal thing. Most Justices either escape the temptation to fall back upon it as a substitute for authority and analysis or are able to sublimate its influence. Others on occasion have openly acknowledged their regard for various federal lower-court trial and appellate judges or counsel.

Chief Justice Vinson's opinion in *Dennis* v. *United States*[17]

17. 341 U.S. 495 (1951). This case sustained the constitutionality of the Smith Act and the conviction of the top eleven leaders of the American Communist Party thereunder. However, it also embodies a classic example of Supreme Court obfuscation of legal principle. The

presents an instance of exceptional deference to the calibre of a lower court and particularly to one of its judges. Research could doubtless turn up other examples varying only in the degree of regard indicated for the court below. However, a single instance is sufficient to prompt one to ask whether constitutional or statutory constructions should be left to turn upon the regard that various Justices have for particular lower-court judges. How is the evaluation of merits to be undertaken? Are the imponderables that determine personal esteem relevant in the resolution of constitutional or statutory litigation? How are the views, personal factors, or other sources of merit causing one Justice to favor the opinions and professional competence of a lower-court judge to be evaluated when other considerations lead a colleague to a different choice? Should not the merits of the reasoning, the relevance of authorities, the weight of evidence, and other judicially cognizable determinants be more important in the definition of individual decisions?

THE CHIEF JUDGE OF THE CIRCUIT

The Chief Judge of the circuit acquires his position through being the senior active judge in years of service on the court. He is administrative head of the circuit, yet he "presides" over the court only when it sits *en banc*, and his influence over his fellow judges may range from great to practically nonexistent. Nevertheless, he has some control over the other judges, both District and appellate, of his circuit. In most courts he can determine the composition of appellate-court panels, and whenever a three-judge special District Court is authorized he also determines what district and appellate court judges will join the permanent judge of the district in which that court is to sit.[18]

---

decision was split six to two, with Justice Clark taking no part in the case. The Chief Justice purported to adopt in his opinion the "clear and present danger" doctrine, but the interpretation given it by Judge Learned Hand, Court of Appeals, Second Circuit, and accepted with praise by the Chief Justice, was a much-altered new version endorsed only by the author of the Dennis opinion and Justices Reed, Burton, and Minton. Justices Frankfurter and Jackson concurred in the judgment of the Court but advanced their own reasons to justify their position, while Justices Black and Douglas rejected the judgment and the new "clear and probable danger" test. In all, four interpretations of the test were set forth, as well as two statements why no form of the test was applicable.

18. 28 U.S.C. section 2281, para. 1.

He is a member of the Judicial Conference of the United States, where he has direct contact with the Chief Justice of the Supreme Court. Between meetings, the Chief Judge of the circuit is in direct touch with the Chief Justice and will most certainly be the medium through which the Chief Justice tries to transmit to the lower courts his views on the conduct of judicial business. Nevertheless, Chief Justice Taft is quoted as saying that "The fate of a Chief Justice in attempting to make District and Circuit Judges do what they are not disposed to do is a difficult one."[19] No doubt their resistance is somewhat stiffened by the righteousness of their cause, for intervention by the Chief Justice, even though reinforced by the prestige and authority of his office, amounts to interference with the routine operation of the lower courts in the name of special considerations.

The Chief Judge of a circuit is empowered to move judges about on temporary assignment between districts within the circuit. Also, upon request from the Chief Judge of another circuit and with the consent of the Chief Justice, he can assign a judge from his own circuit to the requesting jurisdiction. He can make similar response to a like request from the Chief Justice. To relieve a congested docket in his circuit, he can ask for the temporary assignment of a district or appellate judge from outside. Sometimes this is done when a judge in a circuit procrastinates in disposing of cases assigned him because he disagrees with the necessary manner of their decision consistent with precedent.

ASSEMBLIES OF JUDGES

A tighter relationship exists between the two levels of lower courts than exists between them and the Supreme Court. This is illustrated by the relative powers of the Judicial Councils of the Circuit and the Judicial Conference of the United States. The circuit councils are competent to make appropriate rules and to issue orders *binding* on all judges within their respective circuits. Thus, each regional council is authorized to "make all necessary orders for the effective and expeditious administration of the business of the courts within its circuit."[20] But the

19. W. F. Murphy, "Chief Justice Taft and the Lower Court Bureaucracy," 24 *Journal of Politics* 453 (1962), at p. 459.
20. 28 U.S.C. section 332.

national Judicial Conference is a wholly advisory body and has the ability only to formulate proposals and to make recommendations. On its own authority it may not take action or formulate binding rules on the lower courts or their judges.

If the judicial system were genuinely integrated, the supervisory role of the national conference would probably be more formalized, with competence to take binding action and to issue rules whose force extended throughout the judicial structure. But as it stands now, though the national conference's Standing Committee on Rules of Practice and Procedure has a continuing responsibility to study federal procedure, the conference merely reports its *suggestions* to the Supreme Court "to promote simplicity in procedure, fairness in administration, the just determination of litigation, and the elimination of unjustifiable expense and delay."[21]

The Judicial Conference of the United States. The Annual Judicial Conference of the United States is not, however, without significance in intercourt relations. Though presided over by the Chief Justice, the Conference is dominated by lower-court judges. Its membership consists of the Chief Judge of each circuit, an elected district judge from each circuit, and judges from some specialized tribunals. The national conference endorses the procedural rules ultimately binding on federal courts. Acting under authority delegated to it by Congress, the Supreme Court has authority to prescribe (subject to disallowance by Congress) rules for uniform procedures in civil and criminal prosecutions in District Courts. The involvement of the High Court in formulating the rules, however, is nominal, the work of study and preparation being done for the Court in the Judicial Conference. The principal input comes from the Conference's Committee on Rules of Practice and Procedure. However, the Committee works cooperatively with counsel from the judicial committees of the House and Senate, and proposed amendments to rules are submitted to the bench and bar for comments and suggestions. Once prepared, rules are formally proposed by vote of the Justices and they become operable if not rejected by Congress within ninety days. Hence congressional consent is given so as to avoid a presidential veto. Establishment of these common rules has promoted cohesiveness and integration within

21. 28 U.S.C. section 331.

the court system; and the rules have had signal effect in bringing about procedural uniformity.

It is also the task of the national conference to maximize efficient use of the lower courts. To that end, it makes a comprehensive survey of the work records of the lower judges and courts, and ascertains, with the help of the Administrative Office, which tribunals need aid and which are in a position to render it.

The Conference receives from the House and Senate for study, endorsement, or disapproval all proposed legislation affecting the judicial branch. The action of the Conference, of course, is not binding upon the judiciary committees of Congress or upon its houses, but it appears to carry much force with the legislators, who in debate on judicial legislation repeatedly invoke its authority.

Proposed legislation which would affect the lower courts is reviewed in the Conference by a special procedure that has been evolved to provide circuit and district judges opportunity to express their opinions. Before any measure pertaining to the District Courts is recommended by the Conference, it is studied by a committee appointed by the Chief Justice from the membership of the Conference, with at least half of the members being district judges. The report of the special *ad hoc* committee is circulated among *all* circuit and district judges and discussed in the conferences of the circuits. Any actions taken in the circuit conferences on the proposals are reported by the senior circuit judges to the Judicial Conference of the United States. Only when this process of searching analysis is completed does the annual judicial conference submit its recommendations to Congress.

The Conference gives the Chief Justice a forum in which to address all lower-court judges as directly and as forcefully as he will, and some Chief Justices use it in this way. Both Chief Justices Taft and Hughes made clear to the Conference that in the case of manifest failures by a judge to do his duty they were ready to admonish him (albeit tactfully, cautiously, and without giving unnecessary offense). However, Chief Justice Hughes also advocated creation of conferences in the circuits, feeling that primary responsibility for direct supervision of district judges ought to rest there, where it could be exercised more effectively than it could by the more remote Chief Justice. There it does rest, but the National Conference is available for such use as an incumbent Chief Justice can make of it, depending upon his own conception of his role vis-a-vis the lower judges, his personal prestige and that of his office, the reputation of his Court, its support of him, his own powers of persuasion, and whatever else adds to or detracts from the force of his explanations, opinions, criticisms, or suggestions.

At best, the record of the Conference suggests that it is an agent of moderate and restrained reform. Conference positions on issues of systematic change have behind them the collective knowledge, insights, and experience of the assembled lower-court judges. Because of the generally conserving outlook of bench and bar, dramatic, radical reforms are not likely to be forthcoming. The outputs from the Conference to the appellate and district tribunals consist largely of appeals to professionalism and to pride of accomplishment. However, the Conference occasionally has assumed the role of spokesman for lower-court attitudes in reaction to Supreme Court decisions, as when it attacked that tribunal's decisions in the 1950's relating to lower-court use of habeas corpus proceedings while Earl Warren was Chief Justice.

But however deliberate and systematic the Conference's examination of the lower federal judiciary may be, its proposals do not always receive ready acceptance and instant implementation. Some of its momentum for reform can be expected to trickle down to the level of the District Courts, but there the reception it receives is certain to vary according to judicial predilections and experience and to prevailing local conditions. Even though they are backed by supporting evidence, recommendations on such matters as alterations of jurisdiction, creation of new courts, addition of judgeships, or modifications of procedure may encounter resistance, reluctance, hostility, and— occasionally—retaliatory action. A favorable reception for the recommendations of the Conference is not assured below by the formal authority, the prestige, or the weight of evidence above.

Nevertheless, the accomplishments of the Conference have been notable. Many have been achieved largely by working within the existing rules, practices, and organization of the judicial system, with minimum reliance on new legislation. Thus, by utilizing available resources indigenous to the judiciary and the judicial process, the Judicial Conference of the United

States has served to bridge the formal gulf between the Supreme Court and the lower tribunals of the regular constitutional judiciary, but it has done so only modestly at best. It has also served as an agent of accommodation for local sensibilities and interests and even for individual judicial temperaments.

The Judicial Conference was not meant to be an agency for hierarchically integrating the Supreme Court and the inferior tribunals. It does not in a significant way bring the Supreme Court as an institution or its members as individuals into contact with the lower courts or with a large number of their judges. The effectiveness of the Conference is a function of the use made of it. To a considerable degree it depends on the personality of the Chief Justice, and his ability to meet participating lower-court judges and to discuss the problems of the judicial system in a friendly, personal, statesmanlike manner. Nevertheless, the opportunities presented by the face-to-face confrontation between the Chief Justice of the United States and selected lower-court judges are unique within the judicial system, and are valuable for encouraging cooperation, for consulting directly, and for systematizing and explaining matters of common concern on a personal basis.

In its present form, the Conference is an agency by which the persuasive powers of the Chief Justice can be brought to bear on only a limited number of lower-court judges. Those attending may or may not be faithful transmitters of ideas and criticisms, of proposals and their defenses, to their many colleagues below. Stripped to its bare essentials, the Conference seems most usable by its lower-court membership as a device for self-protection, to the extent that its prestige gives it persuasive influence. The Conference generates a sense of unity within the lower levels of the constitutional court structure, but it seems neither to pose a threat to the identity and independence of the individual parts nor to do anything to make a genuine tri-level integrated system out of it.

The Judicial Conferences of the Circuits.   The Chief Judge of each circuit presides over and plays an active role in the annual meetings of the circuit conference, which is composed of the appellate judges, the district judges of the circuit, and representative members of the circuit bar, whose participation in open sessions is encouraged. To the conference may also come the Circuit Justice, whose function it is to report on the work of the Supreme Court.[22] The conferences have become important arenas for the discussion of legislation recommended by the Judicial Conference of the United States and for soliciting opinions of lower-court judges pertaining to it.

Meetings of the circuit conference also provide opportunities for the airing and harmonizing of intra-circuit problems between District Courts and appellate tribunals, between judges, and between the benches of the circuits and the bars of the states within them. The conference is supposed to exercise general supervision over the conduct of business by individual courts and judges and to take whatever measures are thought necessary to remedy problems of judicial operation. However, because the circuit judicial conferences have neither tended to police the performance of trial judges vigorously nor to secure cooperation in the absence of voluntary compliance, the taking of enforcement or supervisory action has usually fallen on the Chief Judge, who is most often extremely reluctant to interfere with District Court affairs. For their part, district judges resent attempts by their judicial superiors to employ compulsory powers to supervise their operations. Therefore, the Chief Judge ordinarily proceeds very informally in his relations with the other judges of his circuit so as not to ruffle smooth relations. But if he is disposed to do so, he can try to employ the judicial conference to police such matters as the disposition of litigation by the circuit's judges, their conformity to the decisions of higher authority, and their regard for litigants' rights.

In a real sense, the values of judicial independence broadly viewed have curbed use of the conference; for here the District Courts' strong tradition of local administrative autonomy is encountered. That tradition makes the conferences reluctant to act and may stimulate in the district judges a resistance to external direction. Admittedly, a bad record for handling the flow of judicial business such as attracts the attention of a conference may be caused by many factors, some beyond the discretionary control of the trial judges. However, some delay may also result from the questionable practices of the local court: for

22. Justice W. J. Brennan, Jr., "The National Court of Appeals: Another Dissent," address delivered before the Circuit Conference, First Circuit, Portsmouth, N.H., 23 May 1973, printed in 40 *University of Chicago Law Review* 473 (1973). The conferences are controlled by 28 U.S.C. section 333.

instance, sloth on the part of the judge; his failure to purge the calendar of old, inactive cases; his too easy willingness to grant delays; or his failure to employ pre-trial modes of disposition. Whatever the cause, the tradition is very strongly felt in many lower national courts that each court "belongs" to its judge, to be run by him according to his preferences and local ground-rules within the limits fixed by the uniform rules of practice and procedure. The feeling that a court "belongs" to its judge is doubtless enhanced by the fact that each judicial appointment is to a particular court rather than to an integrated "bench" drawn upon to man the various tribunals wherever they might be located geographically.

The Judicial Councils.   The semiannual meetings of judicial councils are presided over by the Chief Judge of the Circuit and are composed of all its appellate judges.[23] These meetings may also help harmonize relationships between courts and judges of the federal judicial system, but their contribution to smooth personal relations is more locally focused and indirect than that of the circuit conferences. Their main function is to consider the state of judicial business in the circuits as revealed by periodic statistical data on conditions of dockets, dispositions per judge, and pendency time of cases. The Councils are authorized to take such action "as may be necessary" to remedy any situation of deficiency in the operation of District Courts. For example, they can advise the Chief Judge of the circuit on the temporary shifting of judges between District Courts within the circuit, the advisability of seeking outside assistance from another circuit, or on using pretrial conferences more extensively. Each district judge of the circuit is charged by statute promptly to carry out the directions of the council relating to the conduct of judicial business by his court.[24] Hence, the judicial councils have broad powers for supervising and directing the administration of the district tribunals. But the councils are concerned only with the mechanics of a court's operation viewed as a single wheel in the total machine for administering federal justice. The focus of the judicial councils is local, and their effect upon lower-court/Supreme Court relations is at best attenuated and indirect.

23. For a critical appraisal of the Councils, see "The Circuit Councils: Rusty Hinges of Federal Judicial Administration," 37 *University of Chicago Law Review* 203 (1970).

24. 28 U.S.C. section 332(d).

In 1965 one judicial council undertook a novel course of action against a recalcitrant jurist. Its action was prompted by the difficulty of imposing discipline within a judicial system where the *de facto* separation of the various courts makes the exercise of compulsion by a higher court or judge upon a lower one virtually impossible. The roadblocks to discipline are so numerous and effective that, when a judge has failed to administer the affairs of his office without working harm or hardship to litigants or to the judicial system, the situation, however deplorable, has been without remedy short of impeachment or persuasion. However, in the case of Chief Judge Stephen S. Chandler, United States District Court for the Western District of Oklahoma, the judicial council utilized an innovation to overcome what seemed to be an impasse of personal intransigence growing out of differences between Chief Judge Chandler and his colleagues. Drawing upon its statutory authority to "make all necessary orders for the effective and expeditious administration of the business of the courts within its circuit," the council concluded that under prevaling circumstances Judge Chandler was "unable or unwilling" to perform his judicial duties. Therefore it ordered that no further cases be assigned him and that he act no further on those pending before him. Although the legitimacy of the council's action was widely questioned, Judge Chandler unsuccessfully challenged the council's competence to act as it did by asking the Court of Appeals, Tenth Circuit, and the Supreme Court to intervene.[25]

Although the order issued by the Tenth Circuit was apparently within its authority, it was the product of a procedure that in many respects is less than acceptable. Judge Chandler was afforded no opportunity to make a defense, afforded no hearing,

25. See, for the events of Judge Chandler's experience, *Chandler, U.S. District Judge* v. *Judicial Council of the Tenth Circuit of the United States*, 382 U.S. 1003 (1965), denying application for a "Stay of Order of Judicial Council of the Tenth Circuit," referred by Mr. Justice White, to whom it was made, to the Court; *O'Bryan* v. *Chandler*, 384 U.S. 926 (1966), Certiorari to CCA, Tenth Circuit denied. Reported below in 352 F. 2d 987; *O'Bryan* v. *Chandler, U.S. District Judge*, 338 U.S. 904 (1967), denying motion for leave to file petition for prohibition and/or mandamus; *Chandler, U.S. District Judge* v. *United States*, 389 U.S. 568 (1968), granting petition for writ of certiorari but on independent examination of papers, vacating judgment of Court of Appeals, Tenth Circuit, and remanding with instructions to dismiss mandamus proceeding as moot.

given no notice of the action to be taken against him, and pro-vided with no specification of the charges against him. The order of the circuit did not attempt to oust him from his judgeship, for that it clearly could not do, but it did have the practical effect of negating his competence to judge.

PERSONALITY AND PERSONAL RELATIONS BETWEEN COURTS

Even though the appellate judge cannot avoid placing on his lower-court colleagues whatever stigma is attached to being reversed, he ought to do so with humility, consideration, and respect. There have been occasions when the Justices of the Supreme Court have seemingly disregarded the sensibilities of those lower-court judges whom they singled out for attention, but ordinarily their opinions respectfully indicate to the court below where it went wrong.

Whatever their real feelings about the merits of higher-court opinions, reasoning, or judicial personalities may be, lower-court judges are institutionally obligated to give at least an external appearance of deference and respect. Judge Calvin Magruder, Court of Appeals, District of Columbia, once wrote that his court felt an obligation to "always express a respectful deference to controlling decisions of the Supreme Court, and do our best to follow them. We should leave it to the Supreme Court to overrule its own cases." But Judge Magruder admitted that he had not always refrained from trying to lead the High Court when no clear precedent compelled him to a particular con-clusion. Judge Magruder frankly noted that he did not find pleasure in getting reversed by the Supreme Court. A sense of resentment grew out of his having spent long hours studying a case and writing a well-reasoned opinion only to have his reasoning brushed aside by what appeared to be "a superficial and hastily prepared" opinion. But, Judge Magruder went on to state, initial indignation subsided when reflection suggested that the apparent poor quality of the Supreme Court's opinion might be due to the pressure under which it worked and that were positions reversed the same causes might well produce the same objectionable results.[26]

26. "The Trials and Tribulations of an Intermediate Appellate Court," 44 *Cornell Law Quarterly* 1 (1958).

It seems clear that intercourt relations are in part a function of judicial personality. The aggressive, innovative, imperturbable lower-court judge (who does not mind being rebuffed above while he tries to stimulate growth in the law by prodding his judicial superiors to take a new stand) will not be content to restrain himself to a pedantic or pedestrian application of ancient principles. His efforts will probably earn him little more than the criticism of his more cautious, conservative, and tradition-minded brethren. Others attuned like himself to new views, however, may regard his enterprise as commendable. To the first, he may appear to "rock the boat" and to add unjustifiably to that uncertainty which always characterizes the law and its processes. The second may praise his judicial statesmanship and rate him as one of the most valuable members of the federal lower-court bench.

Yet, while these patterns of attitude and action are commonly felt among judges, the regard in which a particular judge is held by his peers and superiors is probably determined mainly by such things as his demonstrated technical skills and the sound-ness of his reasoning processes. Is the "good" lower-court judge one whose personality impels him to follow placidly along the path of precedent, waiting patiently for higher authority to speak? Or does the "good" judge, especially of the inter-mediate court, owe it to the legal profession and to the Justices of the Supreme Court to throw upon a novel area or problem of law whatever insight he can bring to bear upon the course of legal development? How much deference should be shown by the Supreme Court to the ground-breaking conclusions of an appellate judge?

Although the Courts of Appeals are not primarily public-law/public-policy courts, appellate-court decision-making can give—and on some occasions must give—public-policy implications determinative weight. On such occasions an appellate court has available to it as many options as the High Court does for the disposition of a case on its merits. Also, the variety of precedents present for selection is as great, and the probability of review, though present, is normally slight. In other words, the "mechan-ical decision-making" characteristic of the private-law sector of appellate business can be displaced as occasion demands by as much public policy-making as may be called for in the opinion of the judges of the circuit. Moreover, such public-policy dimensions of litigation as may have emerged during trial or have been perfected on appeal tend to assume a prominence they did not have below, where enforcement of specific legal rules rather than the weighing of broad policy implications is the usual theme.

The function of law as an instrument of social control would seem to impose upon lower-court judges, therefore, responsibility to advocate that version of the rule they believe to be most meritorious. Judge Magruder has indicated his belief that appellate judges should endeavor to persuade higher authority that the decision should go one way rather than another. Moreover, the obligation of appellate judges also extends to those issues of law which, though they *can* be taken to a higher court by the established normal operation of the judicial system, because of their insignificance or narrow focus probably ought not to be taken there. Such questions should be freely and finally dealt with by the intermediate courts. In this way, the lower federal courts are able to provide justice to private parties while the Supreme Court is spared the pressure of claims important only to the parties concerned.

POLITICS AND APPELLATE COURTS

Courts of Appeals are more apt than District Courts to bring to adjudication a greater sensitivity to constitutional doctrine and to the purposes of national legislation and its implementing programs. Their broader jurisdictional areas and the lessened impact of politics and localism upon the appointment of appellate judges make some contribution to that end. Because decisions are rendered by three-judge panels, they can reasonably be expected to bring to the solution of legal disputes greater experience, knowledge, and—perhaps—wisdom than can a single-judge District Court. Decisions by at least two members of a three-judge panel may normally be expected to reassure litigants and the general public concerning the scope and extent of a court's deliberations. The prestige of the tribunal as an appellate body lends further weight to its decisions. The legitimating force of a panel of three appellate judges takes on added significance in cases likely to bring on a drawn-out and disharmonious contest with a state legislature or other local authority. The appellate tribunals can normally be counted upon to be less parochial in their outlook, more free of the pulls of local ties and sentiments and of the obligations of "senatorial courtesy," and hence more representative of a national outlook. Moreover, the selection process has worked with marked success to exclude from the appellate benches the worst of the parochially oriented and interest-serving District Court judges, and it has usually picked men of wide experience, diverse background, and high caliber.

Nevertheless, the appellate courts do acquire identifying personalities. Bloc voting is not unknown, and although evidence is scant with regard to this subject, there is enough to suggest strongly that appellate courts are neither wholly beyond politics nor moved exclusively by considerations of abstract justice.[27] The interests represented and the values held by the members of appellate courts do vary within a court and between different courts, and differences of orientation undoubtedly account in part for the divergent decisions reached in similar cases by the appellate courts of different circuits. Several decades ago, for example, the Court of Appeals, Fifth Circuit, represented those values associated with Southern democracy, especially the area's traditional opposition to organized labor. Its attitudes revealed a strong bias against constraints imposed by a remote national government, particularly against efforts of the National Labor Relations Board to interfere with free relations between management and workers. That latter bias was so pronounced and the tribunal's obstructive tactics so persistent that it was censured by the Supreme Court in 1940.[28] Throughout the 1930's this particular appellate court demonstrated an anti-New Deal, conservative economic and political philosophy of localism, individualism, governmental self-restraint, and states' rights. Its effective leader, Chief Judge Hutcheson, refused to follow the lead of the High Court when it implied a move to curb state power over the licensing and censoring of motion pictures. The Chief Judge's reaction was caused by the fact that in 1915 the Supreme Court had held that a state's authority to license and

27. Identification of blocs is made very difficult by the use of *ad hoc* three-judge panels. However, some consistent patterns of intra-court individual voting have been established by voting behavior analyses, and examination of *en banc* voting has suggested that permanent alignments can be identified in policy areas characterized by high levels of intra-court conflict. Some results can be found in S. Goldman, "Voting Behavior of the United States Courts of Appeals, 1961–1964," 60 *American Political Science Review* 374–383 (1966); "Judicial Performance in the Fifth Circuit," 73 *Yale Law Journal* 90 (1963).

28. *NLRB* v. *Waterman Steam Ship Company*, 309 U.S. 206 (1940).

censor motion pictures intended for local showing was substantially unrestricted, since the activity was "a business pure and simple, originated and conducted for profit" and "not to be regarded . . . as part of the press of the country or as organs of public opinion."[29] Later, however, in 1948, in *United States* v. *Paramount Pictures*[30] the Supreme Court seemed gratuitously to redirect constitutional doctrine by asserting in pure dictum, in an antitrust suit, in the words of Justice Douglas, that "We have no doubt that moving pictures, like newspapers and radio, are included in the press whose freedom is guaranteed by the First Amendment."[31] The words clearly portended that the many state and local censorship and licensing boards that had sprung up between 1915 and 1948 might soon be subjected to First Amendment constraints.

On the other hand, a judge who maintains a pattern of views more compatible with those of the High Court may willingly follow its lead, and if he is one of the select company of appellate judges who have gained the Court's special respect, he may successfully encourage it to move faster in the shaping of new constitutional or statutory law. Such was the role reportedly played by Henry W. Edgerton, Chief Judge of the Court of Appeals, District of Columbia, whose dissenting opinions are thought to have been instrumental in leading the Supreme Court to expand constitutional protection in matters of segregated education, racially restrictive covenants, freedom of individual beliefs, and legislative investigative power. The respect held by the Justices for Judge Edgerton's views is suggested by one study to have been so strong that if he dissented from an opinion of his court, there was a 60 percent greater chance that the Supreme Court would grant review, as compared to a 13 percent chance that it would do so if he agreed with his colleagues to make a majority.[32]

Members of Congress or blocs of them are not above manipulating the intermediate tribunals to attain political ends. National

29. *Mutual Film Corporation* v. *Ohio Industrial Commission*, 236 U.S. 230, 244 (1915).

30. 334 U.S. 131 (1948).

31. Ibid., p. 166.

32. S. Rosenzweig, "The Opinions of Judge Edgerton: A Study in the Judicial Process," 37 *Cornell Law Quarterly* 149 (1952). See also 35 *ABA Journal* 546 (1949) and 38 *Texas Law Review* 145 (1959) for articles on Chief Judge Hutcheson, and 26 *Notre Dame Lawyer* 645 (1950) for an article by him.

as well as more limited considerations make their weight felt. Charles Swisher, noted American constitutional historian, records that a strong motive impelling Congress to create the Tenth Circuit (now consisting of Arizona, Nevada, California, Oregon, Washington, Idaho, Montana, Hawaii, and Alaska) was a desire to link the far West more strongly to the Union as a safeguard against its secession. The ensuing assignment of an Associate Justice of the United States Supreme Court would be, it was felt, a further tie binding the area more firmly.[33] Hence, the Tenth Circuit was created by Congress and a tenth justiceship added to the Supreme Court.

Reorganization of the judicial circuits can be manipulated to influence policy determination by appellate courts, but first regional aggravation must build to a high level and be translated into political pressure. Propitious circumstances for doing this do not often present themselves, but one such instance came to the fore in recent years. The Court of Appeals, Fifth Circuit, had played an instrumental role in promoting protection for the legal rights of blacks in the deep South, and its decisions had gone far to negate the provincialism and localistic opposition of some United States District Court judges in the region. Hence, the Fifth Circuit court became an object of dislike to some Southern Senators and Representatives, state and local politicians, and many residents of the area. It was not thought surprising, then, when rumors began to circulate in the early 1960's that an effort was under way to weaken or destroy its effectiveness as a bastion of civil rights in the "white supremacy" South.

The object was to make the tribunal more attuned to the traditional views of the region. The strategy, based on a heavy burden of judicial business, was as follows. The Fifth Circuit, which consists of the states of Florida, Georgia, Alabama, Mississippi, Louisiana, and Texas plus the Canal Zone, was to be divided into two circuits. The altered Fifth Circuit was to consist henceforth of only Florida, Georgia, Alabama, and Mississippi, all strongholds of political conservativism. Texas, Louisiana, and the Canal Zone were to be made a new circuit. Additional judges were to be assigned to each of the newly organized circuits, the entire process of alteration being justified

---

33. *American Constitutional Development* (Houghton Mifflin, 1943), p. 320.

by the existence of a critical burden of civil-rights litigation produced by the region.

However, disquieting reports began to be heard that the real motivation behind this ostensibly high-minded move to improve this appellate court's administration of justice was a desire to sabotage its work in the civil-liberties area. At that time two of the most liberal-minded judges lived west of the Mississippi River and would therefore stay in the new Texas-Louisiana-Canal Zone circuit. Their influence could then be wholly or partly offset there by newly appointed conservative judges. Removal of the civil-rights liberals from the now-reduced Fifth Circuit, still embracing the "Heart of Dixie," plus the influence of new appointments to that court, would assure that the civil-rights movement in Florida, Georgia, Alabama, and Mississippi would be greatly retarded. Thereafter, most of the relief to be obtained by aggrieved parties in the region of the circuit would have to come from the Supreme Court of the United States. An awakened realization that the old but shrunken Fifth Circuit might be too provincial in its outlook reportedly caused abandonment of the reorganization proposal (although surprisingly it was endorsed by the annual Judicial Conference of the United States at its 1964 meeting).

Eventually a plan was arrived at that provided additional judges for the Fifth Circuit but left its territory unchanged. Four additional judges, who could be selected from anywhere in the United States, were assigned temporarily to help with the overladen docket. In this way, powerful Southern congressional opponents of civil liberties were prevented from securing the appointment of new judges attuned to the conservative viewpoint, and the "principle" that no Court of Appeals should have more than nine permanent judges was not violated.

Naturally, the selection of the four temporary judges had to be carefully handled if the intended purpose of their appointment was to be accomplished. One might suspect that their assignment was subject to considerable pressure from both the pro- and the anti-civil-rights groups.

At any rate, the episode of the Fifth Circuit illustrates the degree to which political considerations may permeate the structure and functioning of the intermediate federal courts. The American Bar Association registered its opposition to this tactic of circuit-splitting advocated by southern Senators and

Representatives on the ground that there are other means of coping with the congestion of courts. The Association saw the effort to split jurisdictions as an inherent threat to the accommodation of local and national viewpoints. The dividing of circuits, as proposed in this instance, tends to make local sentiment increasingly strong at the expense of the national perspective. If carried out freely, the practice could eventuate in single circuits for New York, California, and Texas. This would vest tremendous power in the senior Senator of a one-state circuit, and could create appellate tribunals so parochial in outlook that they would lose their perspective as national appellate tribunals controlling the District Courts.[34]

THE SOLICITOR GENERAL: A NON-JUDICIAL CONTROL ON JUDICIAL APPEALS

Certain contacts of the Courts of Appeals with the Supreme Court are controlled not by jurisdictional statutes or rules of procedure but by determinations made by an official of the executive branch. This official is the Solicitor General, whose office is part of the Department of Justice. Full analysis of the Soliticor General's operations and their impact is beyond the scope of this inquiry. Nevertheless, brief notice of his functions must be taken here because the Solicitor General's office controls the upward flow to the Supreme Court of all litigation in which the United States is appellant or in which it is involved as *amicus curiae*. No case prosecuted by an administrative agency

34. *New York Times*, 27 May 1965, p. 22, col. 3. The problem of the Fifth Circuit is not yet resolved. In November, 1973, a congressional Commission on Revision of the Appellate Court System proposed, *inter alia*, that the Fifth Circuit be divided into two three-state circuits but placed Mississippi into one circuit with Texas, Louisiana, and the Canal Zone. Commission members conceded that implementation of their recommendation would be vastly complicated by the strong opposition of Senator Eastland (D., Miss.), powerful chairman of the Senate Judiciary Committee, which must approve any reorganization, to inclusion of his state in the same circuit with Texas. West Coast judges were also vigorously opposed to splitting California by including its southern portion in a new circuit with Arizona and Nevada but leaving northern California in the company of Montana, Idaho, Oregon, Washington, Alaska, Hawaii, and Guam. See the *Washington Post*, 11 November 1973, p. A8.

of the executive branch[35] (including the prosecuting divisions of the Department of Justice) or by United States Attorneys may be taken by appeal or by certiorari to the Supreme Court without approval from the Solicitor General. That official, Stern reports,[36] exercises his firm control in order to protect the Supreme Court from being engulfed by the flood of appeals and petitions for certiorari that might result if every government prosecutor and agency were free to make its own determinations. The Solicitor General's decisions are designed to ensure that only meritorous actions are authorized. They are intended to preserve compliance with the Court's standards for granting certiorari; to improve the quality of petitions, briefs, and jurisdictional statements; and to coordinate the government's legal arguments on appeal in similar cases being taken to the Supreme Court by different agencies and attorneys.

The Office of the Solicitor General must evaluate appellate business from several points of view, some of which must surely have little to do with the legal merits of the issues raised. Although Stern avers that the Solicitor General performs his function independently of presidential policy and of the Attorney General, it strains credibility to assume that tactical considerations play no part in determining which cases to push and which to hold back, or how to formulate arguments and utilize precedents. Even if one assumes that the Solicitor General does operate wholly above politics, one can be sure that certain strategic calculations must lie behind a request to his office for authorization to seek Supreme Court review on a "showdown" issue. Such questions of judicial gamesmanship include: Are we likely to gain a win on the point of law we want defined? Is this the best case for defining the issue so it cannot be avoided? Is the timing right? What are the potential advantages of a win versus the potential damages of a loss?

The Solicitor's role is illustrated in the recent history of litigation attacking the President's power to withhold appro-

35. Some statutory exceptions to this statement exist, but they are distinctly exceptions to the general rule. Although they may proceed without the Solicitor General's approval, close cooperation usually prevails between the excepted agencies and the Solicitor General's office.

36. See R. L. Stern, "The Solicitor General and Administrative Agency Litigation," 46 *ABA Journal* 154–158 and 217–218 (1960); Burt and Schloss, "Government Litigation in the Supreme Court: The Roles of the Solicitor General," 78 *Yale Law Journal* 1442–1481 (1969).

priated funds from expenditure. Despite the facts that a conflict of the most elemental constitutional powers was at hand and that lower national courts had ruled on ten separate occasions between June and August, 1973, against the power claimed and exercised by President Nixon, no case had gone to the Supreme Court.[37] When, however, the President ordered impoundment of almost six billion dollars appropriated for water pollution cleanup and prevention measures, plaintiffs once again attacked his presumed authority. But, instead of challenging the power of the President to impound in the name of economy, they argued the supremacy of Congress' constitutional authority to fix public policy in statute, to appropriate funds necessary to implement the policy, and to realize legislative purposes free from presidential interference. Again, the water cases were decided at the appellate level against the President's claims. There the matter would have rested had not Solicitor General Robert H. Bork agreed to authorize petitions for certiorari requesting the Supreme Court to reverse the appellate rulings. Reportedly, the Department of Justice, probably in light of the past history of litigation, the magnitude of the clean water program, the public's interest in environmental policy matters, the importance of the national program to state efforts, and the huge amount of money involved, decided to seek a showdown before the Supreme Court on the basic issue of constitutional power. Even then, the Court could dodge the controversy or take jurisdiction - and rule on its merits.

So it is, then, that executive agencies play determining roles in the movement of litigation from the lower courts to the Supreme Court. The Solicitor General's Office acts like a traffic officer in regulating the upward flow of a large portion of the important policy-making opportunities from the lower courts. The Department of Justice exerts additional far-reaching influence over the origin and intercourt movement of policy-

37. The basic issue may be drawn as follows: If Congress legislates to provide and staff, under administration by the Department of Health, Education and Welfare, community mental health centers across the United States and appropriates $52 million to implement the effort and realize its policy objectives, can the President, in the name of economy, order that the money be impounded if doing so will negate the effectiveness of Congress' constitutional power to fix policy in legislation and to appropriate? Can he never order impoundment? Order impoundment at any time on any issue in the name of economy? Do so unless mandatory statutory language precludes his impounding funds in a given instance?

making litigation. This it does by its ability to bring or to refrain from bringing cases, and its power to encourage or dissuade agencies of the executive branch to press or to abandon their use of the courts for policy objectives. It also exerts influence by having its attorneys take over on appeal cases initiated by the United States Attorneys whom it directs. In sum, for whatever ends, the Justice Department can stimulate or retard the development of public-law issues and the intercourt movement of cases according to their implications for policy and their consequences for administrative posture. Lower-court/Supreme Court relations are thus susceptible, in part at least, to becoming policy tools of the executive branch.

CHAPTER 6

The Supreme Court

The most basic fact affecting relations of the Supreme Court with the lower tribunals is that the High Court is passive. It cannot seek cases to decide on its own initiative, but must wait until its authority is activated. Its discretionary jurisdiction then enables its members to filter the flow of cases coming to it, screening out all but those the Justices believe are worthy of their attention.

Nevertheless, when measured by the capabilities of the Supreme Court, the flow of cases and other judicial business from below to the top of the judicial system is considerable, and of necessity much business is disposed of summarily. Of the cases reviewed, a few are finally decided, but most are remanded (sent back down) for further action below according to the rulings or directions of the High Court.

Getting a case to the Supreme Court is not easy. The right to appeal to the Supreme Court is tightly circumscribed by jurisdictional statutes, and, regarded in the hard light of reality, the right to appeal, even when utilized, does not include a right of the appellant to have his case heard fully and disposed of on its merits. Those dissatisfied parties who have no appeal by right must fall back on the discretionary willingness of the Court to call up cases for examination. Because so many requests are received but so few are granted by the Court, voluntary review is more uncertain than the right of appeal is limited. And behind all the formalisms are other no less important conditioning factors unknown to statutes and rules. The road to Supreme Court review is a rough one and is influenced at many turnings by factors having nothing to do with the merits of legal points at issue.

What the Justices do with their formal authority and their informal sources of influence affecting lower courts depends in the last analysis upon what they individually perceive to be proper. In part, their perceptions will have an institutional facet, reflecting a judgment concerning what the Supreme Court ought or ought not to do as part of the constitutional system. Most simply stated, the question is whether the Court ought consciously to engage in an active role as an agency of governance (deliberately shaping the development of public law to make policy, aid the political branches, or engage in "social engineering") or whether it ought to bend every effort to function strictly as a court of law (playing a wholly neutral role, focusing on narrow questions of jural law, ignoring the societal consequences of its decisions, and disregarding their impact upon the ability of the political branches to govern). Every Justice, from the nature of his position, must cognitively or intuitively hold a standard leading him to conclude that the proper role of the Supreme Court is to be either an active or a passive one. But at the same time, every Justice is aware that the need for judicial restraint is constant and that every major question that comes to the Court has a more or less inherent political content.

In part, their perception of what is proper will also have a substantive facet, for individual Justices are rarely, if ever, undeviating proponents of either activism or passivity. The doctrinal area at issue may cause a Justice to respond to the one or to the other perception, shifting according to how he feels about the need to attack or defend the doctrinal status quo. And, needless to say, judicial activism or its opposite is not tied to any particular ideological outlook. "Conservative" judges have been just as willing as "liberal" ones to use judicial position and power to defend according to their convictions what they consider to be "right" public policy or constitutional doctrine.

The Supreme Court is a collegial body, and its determinations to review or not to review lower-court decisions are in part functions of whether the necessary number of its members believe it "ought" to do so. In turn, the Justices' respective decisions to support review reflect their individual ideas about such considerations as whether the merits of the issues raised justify review, whether the doctrinal status quo should be preserved, whether courts should make law or merely interpret it, and whether their court is the proper agency for the undertaking. Individual conclusions produce blocs of like-minded Justices. Hence, the Court's appellate power is exercised through more-or-less temporary aggregations of votes. Although its review powers are one of its principal instruments of contact with and control over the lower tribunals, the occasion and purposes of their exercise are as dependent upon the Justices' predilections, biases, convictions, and intuitions as they are upon their professional attitudes, knowledge of law and procedure, and respect for precedent. Judicial activism or passivism emerges, therefore, as a compound of many and varying ingredients.

It must be presumed, however, that the Justices are aware of the great power that flows from their premier position in the constitutional system and of the vagaries that influence its implementation. A measure of self-restraint is necessary to preserve the difference that must exist between conclusions of judicial judgment and impositions of arbitrary judicial fiat. At any rate, one or the other goes far to affect Supreme Court/inferior-court relationships.

REVIEW BY APPEAL AND CERTIORARI

In a small number of statutorily defined instances, cases move on appeal directly from the final decision of three-judge District Courts to the High Court;[1] and appeal from a Court of Appeals can be taken to the Supreme Court only in two instances.[2] In all other instances, the Supreme Court has discretion as to whether it will grant jurisdiction to matters from the inferior courts. The court *considers*, but it does not *review*, all appeals on their merits. Thus one commentator has concluded that "Jurisdic-

1. Jurisdiction of national courts on appeal may be found in 28 U.S.C. section 1257.

2. These are (1) when a *state* statute or constitutional provision has been invalidated because it is in conflict with a national statute, treaty, or constitutional provision, and (2) when in a case to which a national agency, officer, or employee, or the United States, is a party a national law has been declared unconstitutional. Whenever the constitutionality of a federal law is challenged, the Court must invite the United States to appear to offer argument.

tional statements and petitions for certiorari now stand on practically the same footing, and upon the case made in the former, just as in the latter, may depend the grant of further hearing."[3] Moreover, the policy considerations originally giving rise to the differentiation between review by appeal and by petition for a writ of certiorari have lost their force. There seems to be little reason for retaining appeal.

That fact has had little impact on Supreme Court/inferior-court relationships. Even though appeals turned down by the Justices are treated by them as petitions for writs of certiorari,[4] the door to the Court is not thereby opened appreciably wider, nor are policy issues that have been decided below more easily altered, by resort to one method of entry as opposed to the other.

Although rejection of a petition for review is supposed to imply neither approval nor disapproval of the balance of interests arrived at below and to have no effect upon it, rejection nevertheless can have important results for the interests involved. That the Court's refusal to grant a petition for a review is not based on the merits of the controversy is still the preferred interpretation. The bars and the judges of lower federal courts, however, must find it difficult to accept that construction without question, for the Justices increasingly give expression to their disagreements when petitions are rejected.[5]

Writ of Appeal. Cases in prescribed instances may be taken to the Supreme Court by writ of appeal as a matter of statutory right. If the right of appeal exists, the right of the appellant to review is not dependent upon the specific issues raised by, or

3. H. B. Willey, "Jurisdictional Statements on Appeals to the United States Supreme Court," 31 *ABA Journal* 299 (1945).

4. Congress has undertaken to aid parties seeking review by the Court by providing that if appeal is improvidently taken from a decision of a United States Court of Appeals in a case where the proper mode of review is by petition for certiorari, that alone is not sufficient ground for dismissal; but the papers whereon the appeal was taken shall be regarded and acted on as a petition for a writ of certiorari and as if presented to the Supreme Court at the time the appeal was taken. See 28 U.S.C. section 2103, 1958 ed., supp. 5.

5. E.g., see *Brown* v. *Allen*, 344 U.S. 497 (1953); *Simmons* v. *Union News Co.*, 382 U.S. 384 (1966); *Ferguson* v. *Moore-McCormick*, 352 U.S. 528 (1957); *Cameron* v. *Johnson*, 382 U.S. 741 (1965); *Drews* v. *Maryland*, 381 U.S. 421 (1965); *Travia* v. *Lomenzo*, 381 U.S. 431 (1965); *Carlson et al.* v. *United States*, 418 U.S. 924 (1974); *Sians* v. *United States*, 418 U.S. 926 (1974); *Brown* v. *United States*, 418 U.S. 928 (1974).

the nature of the parties to, the case but is statutorily created. A writ of appeal, however, may be dismissed if the Court finds that it lacks jurisdiction over the case. Jurisdiction may be absent because the case "failed to raise a substantial federal question," because the issue originally raised had become moot, because the appellant failed to docket the case within the prescribed time, or because lower courts had failed to develop an adequate record. Some cases are appealed to the Court that should not be, and justifiably they are dismissed; but because the Justices have the last word on what they will act upon, they can dismiss appeals in order to evade questions they do not wish to decide. In either situation the Justices will not review on appeal. During each term a high proportion of appeals are dismissed or lower-court decisions are affirmed without hearings being held or opinions being written.

Writ of Certiorari. A writ of certiorari is a statutory writ[6] used by a higher court at its discretion to call up for review from a lower court the record of a case or controversy. By its use, a party who cannot appeal to the Supreme Court from the decision of a lower court may petition it to review his case, but he is at the complete mercy of the High Court in its disposition of his request. From the lower national courts an overwhelming proportion of the Supreme Court's appellate business comes up by this means, and virtually all of that comes from the Courts of Appeals.[7] Hence, the screening of applications for writs of certiorari enables the Justices to select from all the "federal" questions that come to it those which in the opinion of at least *four* Justices are of sufficient significance to warrant the Supreme Court's attention.

The odds are high against petitioners obtaining review on certiorari. The rejection rate on petitions often runs in the vicinity of 90 percent, and the complete discretionary character of the writ bestows on the Justices total freedom to grant or deny an application. During the 1973 term Justice Brennan reported that 70 percent of the cases filed were not thought to merit even

6. Controlled by 28 U.S.C. section 1254. The Supreme Court does not actually issue a writ, inasmuch as the petitioner must file the certified record of the lower court with his request for review. Gressman and Stern, *Supreme Court Practice*, 4th ed. (Bureau of National Affairs, 1969), p. 24.

7. Some cases come from the Courts of Claims and of Customs and Patents Appeals. No cases move for review by certiorari from the District Courts to the Supreme Court.

conference discussion, a stage that requires a request from only one Justice. Of those discussed, 60 percent received the votes of four or five Justices, but only 9 percent were unanimously called up for plenary review.[8]

Resort to the process comes from dissatisfied parties; lower tribunals cannot invoke the procedure. As an avenue for lower-court/Supreme Court relationships, certiorari is a one-way street; therefore, the attractiveness of the writ is sharply curtailed by the improbability of its succeeding, for the chances of its failure are significantly enhanced by the writ's having been designed to foster the Supreme Court's control of the cases it will review. To that end, grant of the writ is further curbed by the Justices' determination to make it available upon a very sparing basis. Rule 19 of the Supreme Court formally restricts its issuance to cases presenting "special and important reasons." To illustrate: petitions have been granted because two appellate courts have reached different conclusions in essentially like cases presenting the same question of law; because one or more appellate courts have decided a basic question of national law or right not previously passed on by the Supreme Court; because the Supreme Court desires to invoke its supervisory authority over the lower tribunals; or because a lower court has departed from the binding force of a High Court precedent. These are examples of situations that four Justices thought presented problems sufficiently threatening to the symmetry of national law, or to the harmonious operation of the national judicial system, to impel the Court's intervention; the writ is not available merely to serve the interests of parties. Moreover, the writ operates on ordinary District Courts only through the Court of Appeals, so that certiorari will not reach a trial-court decision, no matter how "substantial" the issues of law or procedure raised by its record may be, unless its decision is first appealed to a Court of Appeals. Only from an appellate decision can a petition for a writ of certiorari be taken.

These conditions defining the availability and use of the writ grow out of the Supreme Court's need to protect its docket. In the process, the disturbing effect of certiorari procedure upon the placid relations between the lower and Supreme Courts is

8. Justice W. J. Brennan, Jr., "The National Court of Appeals: Another Dissent," address delivered before the Circuit Conference, First Circuit, Portsmouth, N.H., 23 May 1973, printed in 40 *University of Chicago Law Review* 473 (1973), at pp. 479, 481.

minimized and restricted to those relatively rare instances when issues are raised whose consequences extend far beyond the immediate facts or parties to the dispute. And because the Supreme Court alone determines when this condition has been met, its image as the apex of a true hierarchy of national courts is perpetuated.

Review of cases by certiorari, however, is influenced by numerous considerations extraneous to their merits as measured by the formal criteria of Rule 19. Grant of a petition may depend upon the Justices' biases for or against the questions raised, their regard for the standing of the lower court, and their estimate of the reputation of the lower-court judges who have previously dealt with the issues. Other factors include their intuitive judgments of timing, public reaction, and the impact of the probable decision upon the Court's public image. Their estimate of public interest in the issues raised, their balancing of public response to inaction versus action, and their calculations of consequences for significant social interests are also important among the myriad influences working on the minds and emotions of individual Justices.

Determination by each Justice of which petitions to support, which to oppose, and which to ignore is and ever will be an innately individual, intuitive matter based on feeling, not on ascertainable rules and objective standards.[9] Concurrence is general that experience on the Court develops an untutorable capacity for distinguishing meritorious from frivolous petitions. Most Justices automatically discard cases presenting questions affecting one or a few persons or a restricted locality, unique issues of conflict or ones unlikely to arise again for many years, and cases raising no federal question or none of sufficient substance to warrant attention. Sometimes, however, the Justices' failure in conference to muster four votes for review, or even one vote necessary to start discussion of a petition's merits, comes from the conviction that the conclusions reached below were correct and should be left unaltered.

Automatic acceptances are almost nonexistent. The Justices have tenaciously refused to call up numerous cases clearly falling within the established patterns of Rule 19 when other considerations were felt to override the formal standards of opera-

9. Ibid., p. 479. Brennan is citing his agreement on this point with his former colleague Justice Harlan.

tion. These were usually policy considerations. For example, neither the question of the constitutional propriety of *de facto* segregation, the many divergences of trial and appellate decisions on the matter, nor an intense nationwide interest in the subject were sufficient to induce the Justices quickly to review and rule on the merits of the basic question and its many satellite issues. It may be that their delay reflected the Justices' acute sense of caution, their desire to have and to profit from maximum input by lower courts, or their determination to let the controversy mature before they injected themselves into the dispute. Petitions for "untimely" review may be passed over in conference in order to give inferior courts the opportunity to bring the diversity of their experience to bear upon an issue or to permit an already roaring constitutional problem to reach full development. One currently sitting Justice is reported to have stated candidly but anonymously that "Even when I am inclined to hear a novel case, I often vote to deny just so we can get more input, more perspective from the lower courts."[10]

What might be called the element of judicial statesmanship may also affect the granting of petitions for writs of certiorari. Without question, the Court could have encouraged public-school desegregation cases to come to it in the decades of the forties and fifties. But it did not, perhaps because the Justices understood that the mood of the American people was not yet sufficiently attuned to reversal of the "separate but equal" doctrine. Also, the Court may have hoped that the political branches of the government would eventually deal with the problem. By dealing first with desegregation or other denials of equality in graduate and professional education (which was more remote from the concerns of the general public and affected relatively few individuals) the Justices forestalled dividing the American people, splitting the Court, and jeopardizing by both consequences its fragile foundation in public acceptance. By putting off the day of decision, slow progressive steps toward the ultimate result were taken through the agency of lower courts and of the Supreme Court, and public education to acceptance of new values was carried out by a gradual movement toward the new plateau.

The Justices' intuitions as to how the Court might rule on an issue if review were granted is also known to influence disposi-

10. Interview reported in *Time*, 11 December 1972, p. 72.

tion of petitions for certiorari. A "bad" decision below might get the four votes necessary for review so that the Supreme Court could have an opportunity to repudiate the lower court's rule of law and to lecture the inferior courts concerning the error of their ways. A decision regarded as "good" might also get the four votes needed for a full hearing if its supporters felt that the Court as a whole would vote to affirm it and thereby notify all lower courts that its rule was to be construed by them as binding. But a decision viewed with horror by four of the Justices—one whose rule they most earnestly felt should be laid to rest—they might vote to reject if they felt a majority on review would vote to affirm. In such a case, the objectionable precedent set below would remain law only within the jurisdictional area of the court that propounded it, and the range of its force would be denied national scope as the law of the land.

Tactics akin to gamesmanship are not unknown in the procedures for handling petitions. By "passing" when his vote is called, a Justice can see which way his colleagues are leaning. By keeping his options open he may be able to create maneuvering room for himself and use his fourth vote to call up a case desired by a subgroup of Justices with which he is most often in agreement. A fourth vote is often picked up from a Justice who gives it because three of his congenial colleagues feel strongly about a petition and need his help. He may consciously or subconsciously expect future return of the favor.

Thus, relations between the Supreme and lower courts based upon certiorari procedure may turn upon nothing more substantial than the vagaries of human temperament. The austere assumption that "the law" and formal rules infallibly govern judicial articulation cannot stand close examination, as any lower-court judge must quickly discover. Ideological differences, nerves frayed and minds exhausted by six or seven hours in conference, personality conflicts, and deep-seated personal prejudices which create interpersonal schisms make questionable the proposition that the granting or denying of review comes from calm deliberation, judicial wisdom, and the rule of impartial, dispassionate law. Although the certiorari process has the great advantage of enabling the Supreme Court to regulate its docket and control the timing of its review, as a means for controlling lower tribunals it is *ad hoc*, random, variable, and highly unpredictable.

Access to the Supreme Court from an inferior tribunal must

also be thought of from the opposite end of the relationship. A party seeking Supreme Court review by either appeal or certiorari is at something of a legal and psychological disadvantage. This is especially true if a party's appeal to the High Court has been taken after losing in both the trial and the intermediate appellate tribunals below. He has had his day in court and one appeal. The decision has gone against him, and to overcome that stigma he must demonstrate that his case presents a significant question worthy of the Supreme Court's time and attention. His chance of winning at the Supreme Court level will be enhanced if the question is one about which the lower appellate courts have divided, or if the Justices do not hold the lower courts in high regard. But a petitioner who cannot induce the Justices to act will probably obtain only a summary affirmance of the lower court's action or a denial of his petition for a writ of certiorari.

SELF-IMPOSED LIMITATIONS

Even should the Court hear argument on an issue, it may utilize some mode of disposition or basis of decision drawn from its various policies of self-limitation. For in addition to the procedural rules the Supreme Court has adopted for the conduct of its business, through the years it has enunciated numerous judge-made norms. Like the formal statutory delineations of jurisdiction, these rules constrain access to the High Court and partially define its relationships with the inferior tribunals.[11]

Note was made above of the constitutional inability of *any* national court to render an expression of opinion in the absence of a genuine case or controversy submitted to adjudication. The Justices, therefore, cannot assist lower tribunals by giving them advice. Its orders to them following review of their decisions on appeal or certiorari are, formally at least, binding instructions, not advice which the lower courts are free to accept or disregard.

Political Questions. In keeping with the doctrine of separated powers, the Justices will abstain from deciding a question that they discover is "political." They will do this in spite of the fact that one or more lower courts may have failed to recognize its "true" nature prior to deciding it. This "constraint," like the

11. On this subject an instructive but brief analysis can be found in J. P. Roche, "Judicial Self-Restraint," 49 *American Political Science Review* 762–772 (1955).

ban on "advisory" opinions, purportedly is a constitutionally grounded but judicially devised, propounded, and invoked rule. Nevertheless, it has been called a subterfuge. It was rejected *in toto* by Justice Holmes,[12] and was labeled "a stench in the nostrils of strict constructionists" by Judge Learned Hand.

The test of "political" is elusive. Several criteria of "political" have been identified, and what is "political" at one period of history may shed its protective coloration and become justiciable at a later time.[13] Since the Supreme Court alone can identify and proclaim what is and is not "political," the formula seems to possess a dubious pedigree. But it has great practical value to the Supreme Court's members, who can find it a convenient way to duck disturbing policy issues that they wish to evade.[14]

Self-imposed limitations of non-constitutional origin have also been generated by the Justices. Because they are required neither by the Constitution nor by the character of judicial power, they may be disregarded by the Justices without any criticism save that of inconsistency. Chief of these are the canons of constitutional and statutory construction. These serve the Justices, lower-court judges, attorneys, and litigants as guidelines for the probable application of judicial power above. The Justices do not adhere to them with anything like perfect fidelity, but these limitations do receive more than mere lip-service from the Justices.

Self-Imposed Canons of Statutory Construction. There are too many of these auto-limitations and their development is too extensive and complex for full treatment here. Mention of a few of them, however, will show the capacity they give the Court to isolate itself against open, easy access from below. Thus, the Court has often refused to pass upon allegedly "important" public-law issues although those issues were fully debated by an inferior tribunal. A statute will not be declared unconstitutional if any reasonable construction of its language can be found that will save it. Of two available constitutional grounds, that should be chosen which is most closely confined to the facts of the case. Only that part of a statute will be struck down that

12. The Justice in opinion once referred to it as "little more than a play on words." *Nixon* v. *Herndon*, 273 U.S. 536 (1927), p. 540.

13. For example, *Colegrove* v. *Green*, 328 U.S. 549 (1946) and its rejection in *Baker* v. *Carr*, 369 U.S. 186 (1962).

14. See J. Peltason, *Federal Courts in the Political Process* (Doubleday, 1955), p. 10.

cannot be saved. The remainder, if it constitutes an intelligible and enforceable whole, will continue in force. A presumption of constitutionality shall attach to every statute and must be overcome by those who allege its invalidity. The sense of a statute is to be determined by the "plain meaning" of its language as conveyed to a person of ordinary intelligence. The Court will not look behind the face of a statute and consider legislative motive.

Self-Imposed Canons of Constitutional Interpretation. Similar canons of constitutional interpretation have been formulated by the Justices. To the extent that these constitutional canons are applied in disposing of cases they both limit the exercise of Supreme Court power and increase the Court's discretion.

For instance, the Supreme Court does not regard itself as bound to consider a constitutional question merely because a lower court did so. A rule of constitutional law broader than is necessary to dispose of the issue at hand will not be construed and applied. A *plaintiff* must rely upon an explicit part of the Constitution and assert his position with supporting authority in detail; general allegations of invalidity will not do. Attacks on questions of enduring vitality must have been timely made in proceedings below and have been pursued on every feasible occasion thereafter. The Court will not pass on a question of constitutional law in advance of the necessity to decide it. All available remedies must be exhausted below before the constitutional issue can be appealed. A litigant may not attack the validity of a statute the benefits of which he has previously enjoyed. The constitutionality of a statute or action is, within limits, independent of its wisdom, fairness, democratic nature, feasibility, or experience.

Thus it must be concluded that if the Supreme Court is to stand in its special place within the American constitutional system, if it is to fulfill the special functions assigned to it (for example, adjusting the relationships of federalism, superintending constitutional proprieties of the three branches of the national government, and guiding the creation and preservation of substantive and procedural rights) it must have a measure of ability to cut itself off from the lower courts. It must possess a certain degree of self-isolation and self-sufficiency; and it must be able to ensure that questions within the special abilities of the lower courts and appropriate for final disposition by them cannot be brought to it.

THE SUPERVISORY POWER OF THE SUPREME COURT

Much of the Supreme Court's competence to control lower courts is based on its ability to review their actions and decisions. By means of review it can hold them accountable for the procedures they employ, for the substantive law they apply, and for other aspects of lower-court conduct. On rare occasions the Supreme Court may even feel compelled to use its inherent power of contempt against a lower-court judge. It is the power of review, however, that links the Court to the rules, law, and procedures of the inferior tribunals.

Withal, the Supreme Court's review power is probably its most extensively used method for instructing the lower courts in the constitutional or statutory law and procedural niceties they are to apply. Processes of appeal and reversal are parts—most important parts—of the internal control mechanism of the constitutional court system. Appeal is an indispensable tool, for instance, for overcoming the effect of a lower court's honest (or willful) misunderstanding of directives from higher authority. There can be no guarantee, of course, that reversal will have immediate effect as a sanction upon the lower-court judge whose decision has been repudiated. Being reversed will have a disciplinary effect upon a lower-court judge only to the extent that he feels an obligation to obey superior authority. Most inferior-court judges *are* sensible of that obligation. If, however, a High Court precedent is strongly felt to embody "bad law," or if personal bias in a given case weighs more heavily upon a judge than does his devotion to judicial duty, reversal of a decision delivered by him may simply stimulate in him a greater determination to struggle for his conception of "right." In such an instance the separation between the Supreme and the inferior court will be widened and the "hierarchical supremacy" of the Supreme Court weakened.

The Supreme Court's relationship with lower courts through its appellate jurisdiction varies significantly according to the subject of litigation. For example, the Supreme Court tends to leave lower-court review of administrative action largely undisturbed, except when it feels called upon to impose new substantive or procedural guidelines for the lower courts to follow. Similarly, the Supreme Court has its constitutional authority to entertain original suits to which a state is a party, but the Justices have made clear their reluctance to do so whenever the states have statutory access to the lower national courts. This is particularly true if similar questions are under adjudication below. The High Court's position is that questions meet for adjudication below should be decided there, that Supreme Court involvement in issues being resolved in lower courts would retard progress there, would preclude full development of arguments and research on the issues there, and would make lower courts noticeably hesitant to decide pending cases promptly when they know that the same questions are before the Supreme Court.

John P. Frank opines that judicial review applied to achieve enforcement of procedural guarantees upon the lower national courts has made a greater contribution to American life and has been more effective than it has as applied to acts of Congress in general.[15] The rights of criminal defendants in federal District Courts have been repeatedly defined and refined within the constitutionally stated procedural guarantees so that accused persons in federal courts are now well protected. In addition, there is that sweeping, all-inclusive guarantee of procedural fairness known as the "due process of law" clause which liberally safeguards the individual caught up in civil or criminal proceedings and broadly reinforces more specific guarantees. Taken together, the use made of these procedural controls constitutes a second source of Supreme Court power over the inferior courts.

Nevertheless, Schmidhauser and others have noted that the supervisory power of the Supreme Court is easily overrated.[16] The Court does, of course, review, and often reverses, decisions of lower federal courts, but a number of practical considerations preclude its doing so on a thorough and sustained basis. The sheer number of actions disposed of in the lower courts limits the Supreme Court's power of ensuring lower-court conformity to its precedents. Moreover, the Court's inclination to police lower-court adherence to its precedents must surely be weakened by its image of itself as not existing to correct errors committed below.

Additionally, the Supreme Court does not preside over the inferior tribunals like a conductor leading the harmonious

15. "Review and Basic Liberties," in Edmund Cahn, ed., *Supreme Court and Supreme Law* (Indiana University Press, 1954), p. 137.

16. J. Schmidhauser, *Constitutional Law in the Political Process* (Rand McNally, 1963), p. 131.

symphony of the law; it does not lead the lower courts from a constitutional score by which all are undeviatingly bound. But neither do relationships between lower and higher courts constitute *merely* a cacophony of legal individualism produced by each judge freely improvising on the score to suit himself.

We have already noted the ambiguity of many High Court rulings and the Court's tendency, even its obligation, to depart from its own precedents. There is nothing to suggest that lower-court judges are blind to ways of slipping out from under the binding force of Supreme Court decisions. Like subordinates in all areas of endeavor, particularly inferiors separated from their superiors by geographical and psychological distance, the lower courts have a certain willingness to follow their superior but they also may tend to exercise as much independence of action as a judge's estimate of a specific situation calls for and will permit.

Effectiveness of the Court's ability to control lower courts will depend also on its own internal unity, its ability to formulate precise rules for lower courts to follow, and its ability to obtain compliance without stimulating resistance.[17]

Perhaps in tacit admission that its control is more limited than it is reputed to be, the Supreme Court apparently accepts the proposition that Courts of Appeals should have wide latitude to decide whether and how to write opinions, particularly when they summarily affirm District Court decisions.[18] Courts of Appeals are required neither by statute, by rules of practice, nor by procedure prescribed by the Supreme Court to write opinions. The Supreme Court seems to feel, however, that when a District Court judge has explored a point at length, the appellate tribunal ought to explain its position whenever it reverses him. Failure of the appellate court to make its reasoning known may induce the Supreme Court (in an effort to avoid federal questions raised by the record) to deny certiorari or to send the case back for further elaboration. Compelling intermediate courts to write opinions helpful to the High Court would be tantamount to compelling them to prepare *amicus* briefs. Such a requirement would increase the workload of the already burdened inter-

17. For an account of the Supreme Court's largely unproductive effort to influence the use of trial juries in District Courts by means of its review power see J. P. Frank, (above, n. 15), p. 131.

18. See Rule 21, Court of Appeals, Fifth Circuit.

mediate tribunals and would curtail their discretion to determine if opinions are required.

Because the Supreme Court has no "self-starter," its ability to control lower courts by use of its review power is in practice at best random and episodic, and seemingly almost casual. In fact, one almost gets the feeling that in order to preserve public confidence its reputation for effectiveness is designed to offset the reality of its partial coverage and sporadic application.

Examples of Supreme-Court Control.   An example or two may suffice to show how the High Court's review operates to control lower courts. The Supreme Court has used its review power to work an important change in an evidentiary rule governing federal District Courts. For example, the Advisory Committee that drafted the Federal Rules of Criminal Procedure considered but rejected a proposal to exclude from evidence confessions made by persons arrested under national authority who had not been taken before a committing magistrate "without unnecessary delay." Nevertheless, the Supreme Court has read into Rule 5(a) of the Rules of Criminal Procedure the meaning that the Advisory Committee refused to state in the rule when it was written.[19] The Court's ruling set up a new decisional basis for lower courts, imposed constraints on federal law-enforcement officers, created a judicially enforceable right for criminal defendants in federal trials, and contributed to congressional enactment of legislation repudiating the judge-made standard.[20]

The many details of federal-court procedure that are regulated by acts of Congress may also fall within the Court's review power. The following extract from the *United States Reports* clearly illustrates how the statutory authority of District Courts to grant writs of habeas corpus came under the review power of the High Court, which employed review to control the procedure of the inferior courts and to amplify the meaning of pertinent standards:

PER CURIAM.

The petitioner, a prisoner in the Pennsylvania penal system, sought a writ of habeas corpus from the United States District Court for the Western District of Pennsylvania. He alleged,

19. *Mallory* v. *United States*, 354 U.S. 449 (1957).
20. Omnibus Crime Control and Safe Streets Act, 82 Stat. 211–225 (1968).

among other things, that his appointed counsel in the state trial which resulted in his conviction had been ineffective, and that he had therefore been denied the aid and assistance of counsel guaranteed by the Constitution. *Gideon* v. *Wainwright*, 372 U. S. 335. The District Court granted Nowakowski a hearing and appointed a lawyer to assist him. Following the hearing and "[v]iewing the record of the trial and the habeas corpus hearing as a whole" the court concluded that Pennsylvania "cannot be convicted of denying effective aid and assistance of counsel to the relator . . . ." However, the District Judge issued the certificate of probable cause necessary to allow a person in state custody to appeal a denial of federal habeas corpus. 28 U. S. C. § 2253.

The lawyers who assisted the petitioner at the habeas hearing were then allowed to withdraw by the District Court. Nowakowski subsequently petitioned the Court of Appeals for the Third Circuit to allow him to appeal *in forma pauperis* from the District Court's denial of relief. He also asked to be allowed to proceed in the Court of Appeals on written briefs and sought the appointment of counsel. That court denied the petition in the following order:

"Upon consideration of appellant's petition for leave to proceed in forma pauperis and to file handwritten briefs; and for appointment of counsel in the above-entitled case;

"It is ORDERED that the petition be and it hereby is denied."

Following the Third Circuit's denial of Nowakowski's petition for rehearing, he sought a writ of certiorari from this Court. It was granted, as was his motion to proceed *in forma pauperis*. 384 U. S. 984.

We hold that the Court of Appeals erred in denying the petitioner the right to appeal after the District Judge had issued a § 2253 certificate of probable cause. It is established law that a circuit judge or justice entertaining an application for a certificate should give "weighty consideration" to its prior denial by a district judge. *Sullivan* v. *Heinze*, 250 F. 2d 427, 429; Sokol, Federal Habeas Corpus § 17, at 94 (1965). Cf. *In re Woods*, 249 F. 2d 614, 616. But when a district judge grants such a certificate, the court of appeals must grant an appeal *in forma pauperis* (assuming the requisite showing of poverty), and proceed to a disposition of the appeal in accord with its ordinary procedure.

The order of the Court of Appeals for the Third Circuit is therefore vacated and the case is remanded for further proceedings consistent with this opinion.[21]

Revisions and piecemeal modifications must be introduced into the formal rules whenever the need becomes apparent. The High Court must and does supervise their content and implementation so that rigid encrustations of detail do not stultify their value. The Court exercises its supervisory powers to preserve procedural flexibility. Changes must be the result of deliberation and purposeful modification, not of a slow accretion of layer upon layer of hardening details.

It is then a major function of the Supreme Court to *observe* the procedural rules in continuous operation and to facilitate their controlled application according to the needs of lower-court practice. It is a work of mutual benefit to all concerned in which the lower judges have an obvious vested interest, and it is bolstered by the great prestige and leadership of the Court.[22]

In addition to clarifying the rules of federal procedure, the Court has created rules of evidence and other standards for governing lower courts. This it has done by using its review power to amplify the constitutionally guaranteed rights of the criminal defendant, and also to generate norms of procedural due process applicable to lower-court activity. Thus, it has ruled that "In the exercise of the Court's supervisory power and under the peculiar power of federal courts to revise sentences in contempt cases, it is ruled that criminal contempt sentences exceeding six months may not be imposed absent a jury trial or waiver thereof."[23] It has also ruled that evidence may not be admitted by a district judge if it was wrongly seized by a state law-enforcement officer and turned over by him to a federal prosecutor for use in a criminal case before a District Court.[24] The list of rulings having like effect upon lower courts could be extended almost interminably.

An Inherent Supervisory Power? Although the Supreme Court since the 1790's has had a congressional mandate to

21. *Nowakowski* v. *Maroney*, 386 U.S. 542 (1967).
22. This subject is explored at greater length in A. Holtzoff, "Judicial Procedure Reform: The Leadership of the Supreme Court," 43 *ABA Journal* 215 (March 1957).
23. *Cheff* v. *Schnackenberg*, 384 U.S. 373, 380 (1966).
24. *Elkins* v. *United States*, 364 U.S. 206 (1960) overturned the "silver platter" doctrine.

supervise the lower courts, in 1943 in *McNabb* v. *United States*[25] the Court used language to suggest that it also possessed a general supervisory power based on the nature of the judicial system and upon its own position at the peak of the court structure. This power of the Court has been referred to as "inherent" and is thought to be another and major reinforcement for the image of the constitutional court structure as an integrated, homogeneous, and truly hierarchical system of superior-subordinate judicial relationships.

The existence of such a power is debated by some authorities, but its possession and right of exercise have been historically conceded in other judicial systems. The formal power conferred by Constitution and statute is in practice entwined with the "inherent" supervisory power, as is noted in this statement from the opinion of *McNabb* v. *United States*:

> . . . the scope of our reviewing power over convictions brought here from the federal courts is not confined to ascertainment of constitutional validity. Judicial supervision of the administration of criminal justice in the federal courts implies the duty of establishing and maintaining civilized standards of procedure and evidence. Such standards are not satisfied merely by observance of those minimal historic safeguards for securing trial by reasons which are summarized as "due process of law" and below which we reach what is really trial by force. . . .
>
> The principles governing the admissibility of evidence in federal criminal trials have not been restricted, therefore, to those derived solely from the Constitution.[26]

Hence, the Supreme Court can use this supervisory power over the lower constitutional courts to impose standards of procedure on them more stringent than are required by the considerations of elemental fairness demanded by due process of law. The Court's new capacity to control can be invoked by it in civil or criminal proceedings to remedy defects arising from unfair or inequitable practices, and, absent controlling statutes, this can be done without substantial limitation.

The Court has made clear that it intends to use its supervisory capacity to protect interests broader and more far-

25. 318 U.S. 322.
26. Ibid., pp. 340, 341.

reaching than those of the litigants only. It does not confine its examination of lower-court procedure to the effect that objected-to practices have on the rights of parties, but goes beyond this to implement a generously comprehensive supervisory outlook. Thus, in a case involving offensive jury-selection procedures employed in a federal District Court, Justice Douglas asserted that "The injury is not limited to the defendant—there is injury to the jury system, to the law as an institution, to the community at large, and to the democratic ideal reflected in the practices of our courts."[27] Use of the inherent supervisory power has resulted in the creation and enunciation by the Supreme Court of rules that are in effect judicially legislated for general application to the lower tribunals.

Vigorous use by the Supreme Court of its supervisory power since 1943 has provided it with an extremely flexible instrument for control of lower courts. Its ability to oversee lower courts in the name of the "democratic ideal reflected in the practices of our courts" gives it a vast and undefined range of supervision. Its use of this supervisory authority has enabled it to escape the limits of due-process control and left it free to impose more exacting standards on the lower courts. Of course, this capacity, like its statutory rule-making power, is subject to congressional disallowance. Nevertheless, it has been suggested that this very fact may make the Court bolder in its supervision, for should Congress reject a judicially devised and imposed supervisory standard, Congress would bear the brunt of whatever criticism might result.[28] Yet, formulation of a standard is one thing, and securing its wholehearted acceptance and implementation below is quite likely to be another.

INFORMAL INFLUENCES ON LOWER COURTS

Apart from formal procedure and jurisdiction, other influences affect the flow of cases from lower courts to the Supreme Court. As was noted above, the Supreme Court is dependent upon the initiative of dissatisfied parties who seek its aid. However, the willingness of an appellant to push a constitutional or statutory

27. *Ballard* v. *United States*, 329 U.S. 188, 195 (1946).
28. A more detailed discussion of this development can be found in Note, "The Supervisory Power of the Federal Courts," 76 *Harvard Law Review* 1556 (1963).

principle through the judicial system to the Supreme Court depends upon his resolve, nerves, persistence, and purse. As a litigant before the trial court he has already endured a heavy financial outlay and strain of uncertainty. Once a decision is had, the temptation must be great to accept it, especially if half a loaf has been won. And should the litigant avail himself of intermediate review, he can gain a second one before the Supreme Court only by bridging the gulf of technical considerations that separate it from the lower courts and by steeling himself to further expense and uncertainty. Hence the ability of the Supreme Court to carve out a broad policy issue of constitutional significance may depend on little more than a would-be appellant's state of mind and purse.

The Supreme Court, however, is not entirely helpless. It can lead the lower tribunals by persuasion or order; it can reprimand and goad them. Occasionally it gives them unsolicited advice in advance of litigation, leaving no doubt about where it will stand if a projected course of events should occur or an anticipated modification of legal principle mature.

But, as policy demands and occasions permit, the lower tribunals can try to push the Supreme Court to act. For the High Court depends upon them to implement its orders and give meaning to its enunciated principles of law. Thus lower-court decisions can be deliberately shaped to elicit responses from the High Court on matters where controlling principle is vague or nonexistent.

Supreme Court reliance upon inferior courts to carry out the practical effects of its public-policy decisions is often an uncertain means for achieving their optimum implementation. In the second *Brown* v. *Board of Education*[29] case, the High Court seems to have overestimated the commitment of lower-court judges to its precedent and their willingness to resist local pressures by enforcing the new standards of racial equality. The ability of lower courts to implement Supreme Court decisions varies according to how enthusiastically the new policy is received by the public, the number of persons affected, their ability to resist, and their visibility. Implementation is usually automatic and independent of lower-court involvement when a ruling affects a single highly visible public official, as when

29. 349 U.S. 294 (1955).

President Truman promptly implemented the Court's decision in the steel seizure case.[30] (Governors Faubus and Wallace, however, supplied two instances in recent history when this proposition did not operate.) Securing effect is much harder if the policy is not popular or it involves a large number of anonymous bureaucrats or members of semi-autonomous units such as school boards or commissions.[31]

If all other avenues of direction from above fail, the Supreme Court can threaten to assume jurisdiction over a subject. It can simply in effect take over jurisdiction of the substantive issues by the artful employment of its review powers. It can also accomplish this by inducing Congress to modify its statutory jurisdiction so that the new subject matter is incorporated.

The Justices have often given the lower courts much leeway in implementing vaguely spelled out statements of policy in newly emergent and undefined areas of social conflict. Under such circumstances, the inferior tribunals have been given virtual blank checks to break new doctrinal ground. On the other hand, the High Court has also recalled delegated authority that the inferior courts did not use as anticipated or directed from above.[32]

Rarely do lower-court judges flout the ethics, traditions, amenities, and formal attributes of their positions to resist the prestige of the High Court. Not only would their overt repudiation of higher authority bring sanctions to bear against them from within the judicial and legal systems, but such unseemly behavior might arouse public hostility or stimulate remedial action by the legislative branch.

In their turn, the Supreme Court Justices owe to the judges of inferior courts an obligation not to treat their decisions disrespectfully. Trial- and appellate-court decisions are normally reached after much study and deliberation. Except when an intervening opinion of the Supreme Court clearly indicates the ground on which decision must rest, or when the High Court is forcefully indicating its displeasure with a lower court or

30. *Youngstown Sheet and Tube Co.* v. *Sawyer*, 343 U.S. 579 (1952).

31. Beaney and Beiser, "Prayer and Politics: The Impact of Engel and Schempp on the Political Process," 13 *Journal of Public Law* 475–503 (1964).

32. S. Krislov, *The Supreme Court in American Politics* (Macmillan, 1965), p. 19.

judge, it owes to the lower courts a carefully reasoned and full opinion of the grounds for its conclusions. Nevertheless, in the opinion of many critics, reversal, affirmance, or dismissal of lower-court action by the Justices too often takes the form of an abrupt and unenlightening summary action.

The deference owed by the Justices to decisions of lower-court judges should be based not merely on consideration for fellow wearers of the judicial robe or regard for their tender sensitivities. There should also be awareness that the law and society are mutually dependent, and that the lower courts are closer to, and probably more accurately reflect, the competing interests and values struggling for recognition in society. It is within the socioeconomic system that law and the courts must operate, and their existence depends ultimately upon the regard in which they are held by the populace. Neither Supreme nor lower courts should act to jeopardize the good standing of all.

Though the Supreme Court and Congress control the jurisdiction of lower tribunals and thereby the accessibility of parties to them, ultimate responsibility for supervising observance and implementation of these limitations rests on the High Court. But the Justices may feel that access to the courts below should be as open as possible to litigants and that the courts should be as procedurally unencumbered as possible, and the Court may therefore not perform its function with maximum vigor. For example, many cases have a "federal question" slumbering undeveloped within their substantive or procedural aspects. To become vital, the issue needs only to be recognized and nurtured. But the Supreme Court has interpreted somewhat permissively the "federal question" principle, and despite the Courts' character as a public-law tribunal it does not insist that such issues must be fully developed below. Of course, an element of self-interest is present in the matter, for if the lower courts were required to accept *every* case that presents a federal question, the resulting glut of litigation would engulf the system.

The mere presence of the Supreme Court influences the conduct of lower tribunals. The possibility of review, coupled with the fact that certain standards and attitudes are known to exist in the minds of the Justices, can be sufficient to cause a lower court to refrain from acting in a contemplated way or from acting at all. Hence lower courts are moved to remain constant with Supreme Court positions, known or anticipated, not only because of past assertions of authority over them but also because of the possibility of future assertions. Therefore, policy determinations by lower courts may result from nothing more than the fact that the Supreme Court is there and available. That the Court does, in fact, call the lower courts to account serves to emphasize further its continued presence and vitality.

The Supreme Court can exert significant influence over litigation brought into lower courts. From time to time it has invited appropriate parties to initiate litigation for suggested purposes, as in school desegregation and legislative reapportionment actions. Conversely, it has also discouraged litigants from bringing certain types of legal questions below. The Court has effective ways by which to communicate its willingness or unwillingness to extend old principles or formulate new ones.

THE EFFECT OF THE SUPREME COURT'S DOCKET

The Supreme Court's workload also practically determines its relationship with lower courts. Unimportant docket items currently make up a large part of its business, and absorb its time out of proportion to their significance. A constant increase in the business brought to it eats into the time available for evaluation of cases and petitions and forces the Court to be ever more selective in identifying the matters it will attend to. An estimated seventy cases per week now come to the Court. This growing volume of business further isolates it from the inferior courts, magnifies its character as a public-law court, and tends to make more and more lower-court actions final.

Congress has never interpreted the jurisdictional statements of Article III to mean that every final action of an inferior court has to be appealable to the High Court. And since the Supreme Court was brought into existence, the growth of its business has been paralleled by a congressional reduction of open access to its dockets in order to maintain a manageable workload.

Since assuming his position, Chief Justice Burger has zealously advocated procedural reform and modification of the Court's position in the system of national courts. He cites the long workweek and the steadily growing caseloads as factors that imperil the Court's ability to fulfill its fundamental role as, among other things, judicial supervisor of the national court system. To shore up his contention, the Chief Justice makes emphatic that the Court—without significant change in its jurisdiction, procedures, or size—dealt with 1,100 cases in 1942 and 4,500 in 1972, and that by 1980 it will be required to handle an anticipated 7,000.

According to Chief Justice Burger, within two weeks of the opening of the 1972 term the Justices disposed of 824 cases on which they did not wish to hear full argument; of that number, 708 were disposed of during one conference period.[33] At a subsequent conference in December the Justices examined 247 cases and determined whether or not to grant full hearing. Although these numbers included many cases that originated in the judiciaries of the states, those coming up from inferior national courts were also present and were caught up in the same harried procedures of disposition.

PROPOSALS FOR STRUCTURAL CHANGE

Concern over the Court's diminishing ability to carry out its historical and essential functions has produced many proposed remedial measures.

A "Mini-Court." In December, 1972, another remedial measure was projected when a committee appointed by Chief Justice Burger recommended that a National Court of Appeals —a "junior" Supreme Court—be created between the existing Courts of Appeals and the High Court. It would have consisted of seven members chosen on rotation from among appellate-court judges, and, if created, would have taken over from the Supreme Court its burden of screening all actions brought to its dockets from below. The proposed mini-Court would sift through the cases, rule on some itself, refer the most significant to the Supreme Court, and dispose of the remainder out of hand. Of the 4,500 petitions for review now filed annually, only an anticipated 400 to 500 would be passed upward; out of that number, the Supreme Court exercising its present broad discretion might select a third for review and decision. However, the proposed "junior" Supreme Court was regarded as such a potential rival to the place and functions of the Court in the judicial and constitutional systems that a storm of objections

33. As reported in *Time*, 30 October 1972, p. 82. The large numbers are typical, however, of the output of the first conference of a term of court. At that time clearly frivolous and non-meritorious petitions screened over the summer recess were disposed of because not even one Justice desired to talk about them.

from judges, lawyers, Justices, and bar associations brought about abandonment of the plan.[34]

A Supreme Court "Lower Chamber."   A more viable proposal has been advanced by the Advisory Council on Appellate Justice. The Advisory Council consists of thirty-three of the most prominent lawyers, law professors, and judges in the country and wields great influence within the legal community. In February, 1974, it proposed creation of a nine-member "lower chamber" of the Supreme Court to decide cases or classes of cases sent to it by the Justices. The decisions of the lower chamber would have nationwide force. They would be rendered by judges from the Courts of Appeals serving seven-year terms on the new tribunal, at the end of which they would resume their seats below.

The new lower chamber would decide two categories of cases: challenges to state criminal convictions and cases involving hundreds of questions on which Courts of Appeals have handed down conflicting decisions. Under existing conditions the Court lacks time to reach them all, and inconsistencies of law may go unresolved for many years. Valuable time could be saved for the Justices if Congress assigned the new appellate chamber to review whole categories of cases such as tax disputes, bankruptcy proceedings, diversity suits, and petitions for writs of habeas corpus, thereby freeing the Court to perform its public-law functions more extensively. Permitting the Court to continue in its historic role and leaving the Court unimpaired control of its docket, this plan would provide nationally binding, final rulings on hundreds of important conflicts of law that now escape review. This plan is similar to one sponsored by the American Bar Association, a fact that might give it a better chance of adoption.

An Appellate Division.   The ABA plan was also designed to counter the objections against the mini-court. It called for a national division of fifteen judges to be created within the present appellate court system. This Appellate Division would

---

34. Reported in the *Washington Post*, 21 December 1972, p. A10. See also A. J. Goldberg, "Changing the Supreme Court: Do Its Cases Need Screening?" *Current*, March 1973, pp. 6–10; the reply to it by Alexander Bickel, "Changing the Supreme Court: A Case in Favor of Reform," *Current*, April 1973, pp. 11–14; and Justice William J. Brennan, Jr., "The National Court of Appeals: Another Dissent," 40 *University of Chicago Law Review* 473 (1973).

hear designated categories of litigation such as tax cases and appeals from national administrative agencies and state courts, and it would determine which should be heard by the Supreme Court. Decisions by the Appellate Division would become final after ninety days if the Justices did not exercise their option to review during that period.

Specialized Appellate Courts. An older, less controversial plan would leave unaltered the constitutional and historic positions of the present Court as they have developed and as they fulfill public expectation. Under this arrangement all applications for review would, as now, go to the Court. There they would be reviewed to identify the legal questions raised, and would then be referred to one of a number of yet-to-be-created specialized courts for final judgment or decision. Special tribunals might be set up to take jurisdiction under criminal, labor, antitrust, interstate commerce, taxation, patent, and other specialized areas of national law. Each court would have exclusive national appellate jurisdiction in its specialty, subject only to Supreme Court review in selected instances. This plan would increase specialization in appellate jurisdiction, eliminate the need for Supreme Court Justices to pass on technical aspects of cases beyond the range of even their expertise and experience, and be more palatable to the conservatively-minded legal profession as a whole. It would leave the Court in full control of its docket and would preserve its image as dispassionate defender of the Constitution, chief arbiter of American federalism, and champion of individual freedom. It would, presumably at least, permit the Supreme Court to devote its full time and energy to supervising administration of the lower judiciary and to umpiring the system of national public law.

But specialized courts, their detractors argue, represent only a partial solution to problems of the judiciary. They also argue that specialized courts will produce overspecialization—judicial "tunnel vision"—in its judges by virtue of long service with a narrow focus, and that recruitment of judges will present difficult problems. Creation of these courts was carefully considered and rejected by the Commission on Revision of the Federal Court Appellate System, whose principal recommendation is considered next.

A National Court of Appeals. In mid-1975, the Commission on Revision of the Federal Court Appellate System proposed establishment of a National Court of Appeals.[35] With one-half the Commission's members chosen from Congress and endorsement of the new court by five members of the Supreme Court, implementing legislation was virtually assured of serious consideration by Congress. Because the proposal is the one most likely to be adopted, we will take an extended look at its features.

The new court would consist of seven judges appointed in the established way, who would sit only *en banc* and who would render decisions binding on all lower national courts unless negated by the Supreme Court. Its jurisdiction would consist of cases transferred to it before decision by Courts of Appeals, the Court of Claims, and the Court of Customs and Patent Appeals (transfer jurisdiction), and cases referred to it by the Supreme Court from those brought up on appeal or by petitions for writs of certiorari (reference jurisdiction). The National Appellate Court would be required to give full plenary treatment and decision to cases referred by the Supreme Court from those appealed to it. The Supreme Court could refer cases from its certiorari list "with instructions" to decide them on their merits, or it could simply make open-ended referrals, leaving to the National Court of Appeals selection of ones to decide or reject. Reference jurisdiction would leave the Supreme Court free, as it now is, to control its docket; but it would have the new option of referring cases it thought important, but could not or would not handle itself, to the National Court of Appeals. Cases taken to the Supreme Court on appeal could also be referred to the National Court, which would be required to give plenary treatment to each one. Every decision by the National Court would be reviewable on certiorari by the Supreme Court. Thus access to the Court would be as open as it is under existing arrangements.

It is alleged that creation of a National Court of Appeals would produce certain advantages. First, it would not cut the Supreme Court off from litigants and lower tribunals more than it is now isolated. Second, it would leave the High Court in full control of its docket. Third, it would permit speedy and efficient resolution of issues over which two circuits have disagreed, and do this without burdening those courts, litigants, or interests with additional cases that could not resolve the questions.

35. Material in this section was drawn largely from A. Leo Levin, "Do We Need a New National Court?" *Trial*, January 1976, pp. 32–39.

Fourth, it would permit resolution of hundreds of issues decided in the appellate courts but left unreviewed because the adjudicative capacity of the Supreme Court had been exhausted. Fifth, it would augment the appellate capacity of the national court system to render authoritative decisions on important recurring nonconstitutional issues of national law. Sixth, it would eliminate relitigation in the circuits of issues, each authoritative within its jurisdictional area, by parties who are forum-shopping in the hope of obtaining a favorable ruling. Seventh, it would increase the capacity of the national appellate courts to inject greater clarity and uniformity into national law. Eighth, it could be an effective instrument for fixing basic principles of national law arising out of many intricate national statutes, and it could thereby eliminate the need for litigation brought to clarify the law and assure judges, lawyers, and clients that intercircuit conflict will not develop.

The proposed National Court of Appeals, however, has sparked some opposition. Its critics allege that first, by interposing a new level of court between the appellate courts and the Supreme Court it will diminish the status of the intermediate courts and their judges in the minds of the public and the legal profession. Second, it will bureaucratize the administration of national justice by creating another web of complex intercourt relationships. Third, the Supreme Court will have to spend as much time on referrals and on review of petitions for certiorari after the National Court is created as it now spends on appeals and petitions. Fourth, creation of another court should be a measure of last resort to be taken only when other, and as yet untried, measures of reform have proven unsuccessful. Fifth, the contemplated transfer jurisdiction would bypass Supreme Court scrutiny of cases and would permit unscreened issues of all kinds to go directly to the National Court, checked only by the possibility of post-decisional Supreme Court review on certiorari. Sixth, the anticipated advantages of the court's creation are too speculative to justify the disruption of the status quo that will result. Seventh, lawyers and courts can endure some unresolved legal conflicts until the Supreme Court thinks they are important enough for it to decide. Eighth, the fact that only the Chief Justice and Justices White, Blackmun, Powell and Rehnquist endorse the National Court, and even then with numerous reservations, suggests that its proclaimed merits are disputable. Ninth, the National Court will add to government by judicial order at a time when the country's temper requires less, not more, judicial control. Tenth, it will create a second "supreme" court that will rival the constitutional High Court, impair its historic roles, and diminish its stature.

The matter at this writing pends in Congress. Opinion over the Commission's proposal is clearly divided, with five of the Justices cautiously supporting it and four cautiously opposing it in the Supreme Court itself. All spectators urge congressional deliberation. With half of the Commission's membership drawn from the House and half from the Senate, the matter is almost certain to receive serious attention from Congress. Only time will reveal what transformation of the existing court system will be produced if Congress creates the National Court of Appeals.

CONTROL BY WRITS

In exceptional situations the Supreme Court can use certain extraordinary orders in the form of writs against lower courts.[36] But the Justices have emphasized many times that the availability of these remedies is severely limited by controlling rules, decisions, and practices. None of the writs, for instance, issues as a matter of right to the party seeking relief. Instead, their issuance is controlled by the sound discretion of the High Court. Their use is not permitted as a short cut for avoiding the delay and expense of normal, established channels of review and appeal.

But most significantly, "Mandamus, prohibitions, and injunctions against judges are drastic and extraordinary remedies."[37] Only highly unusual and special circumstances will justify their issuance against fellow judges. Moreover, a party who seeks an extraordinary writ against a judge must assume the burden of demonstrating that it should issue. He must show that the actions he wishes the Justices to control below do not fall within

36. 28 U.S.C. section 1651 states simply that the Supreme Court "May issue all writs necessary or appropriate" in aid of its "jurisdiction and agreeable to the usages and principles of law." Under that authority the Court is competent to issue writs of mandamus, quo warranto, prohibition, and injunction to aid it in making its jurisdiction effective.

37. *Ex parte Fahey*, 332 U.S. 258, 259 (1947).

the accepted range of discretionary action available to lower-court judges.

Accordingly, use of these formal sanctions to coerce compliance by a lower-court judge is virtually unheard of. Their use runs the risk of hostility, indignation, and resentment on the part of the inferior judges who are the targets of coercion, and perhaps that of their sympathetic colleagues as well. In fact, the Supreme Court has shown great reluctance to take any measure outside of the regular review processes that could be construed as directed at individual judges below, and it has generally restricted use of its coercive powers over the lower courts to making broad standards and rules for the impersonal guidance of judges.

ORDERS OF THE COURT

The traditional and still-prevalent way that the Supreme Court directs a lower one is by issuing an order having mandatory force. Several forms of orders are available. Which one is employed depends on the objective that the directing authority seeks to bring about below.[38] Except by issuing its orders, the Supreme Court has no formal way to contact the lower courts or to direct its authority to persons or groups party to, or associated with, particular cases and controversies. Examples of its orders are easily found in the *United States Reports*. For example, an opinion handed down in a case decided after argument concluded:

> The judgment of the Court of Appeals upholding the dismissal of this action is therefore reversed, and the case is remanded to that court for further proceedings consistent with this opinion.
>
> *It is so ordered.*[39]

By its orders the Supreme Court notifies lower courts that certiorari has been denied:

38. Each Justice of the Supreme Court in his role of Circuit Justice can issue proper orders on his own authority to the courts of his circuit. Such orders do not originate from or share in the authority of the Supreme Court, and by vote of the High Court can be vacated. Hence, they are not included within this discussion.

39. *Honda, et al.* v. *Clark*, 386 U.S. 484, 502 (1967).

No. 1048. KEY v. UNITED STATES. C. A. 6th Cir. Certiorari denied. *G. Edward Friar* for petitioner. *Solicitor General Marshall, Assistant Attorney General Vinson, Beatrice Rosenberg* and *Mervyn Hamburg* for the United States. Reported below: 371 F. 2d 421.[40]

or that leave to file for designated relief has been acted on:

No. 72–5768. PENNA v. NIXON, PRESIDENT OF THE UNITED STATES, ET AL. Motions for leave to file petitions for writs of mandamus and other relief denied.[41]

or to note probable jurisdiction:

No. 72–459. SLOAN, TREASURER OF PENNSYLVANIA, ET AL. v. LEMON ET AL.; and

No. 72–620. CROUTER v. LEMON ET AL. Appeals from D. C. E. D. Pa. Probable jurisdiction noted. Cases consolidated and a total of one hour allotted for oral argument. These cases to be argued immediately following consolidated cases Nos. 72–694, 72–753, 72–791, and 72–929 [immediately *infra*]. Reported below: 340 F. Supp. 1356.[42]

or to grant certiorari:

No. 72–822. RENEGOTIATION BOARD v. BANNERCRAFT CLOTHING CO., INC., ET AL. C. A. D. C. Cir. Certiorari granted. Reported below: 151 U.S. App. D. C. 174, 466 F. 2d 345.[43]

Some decisions reached after full hearing and with written opinion are self-executing and need no order. Thus having heard argument on appeal in *Roe* v. *Wade* from the U.S. District Court for the Northern District of Texas, the Court disposed of the issues as follows:

The judgment of the District Court as to intervenor Hallford is reversed, and Dr. Hallford's complaint in intervention is dismissed. In all other respects, the judgment of the District Court is affirmed. Costs are allowed to the appellee.

It is so ordered.[44]

40. 386 U.S. 982.
41. 410 U.S. 907.
42. Ibid.
43. Ibid.
44. 410 U.S. 113 (1973).

THE PROBLEM OF SUMMARY DISPOSITION

An overwhelmingly great proportion of the petitions, appeals, and other items of appellate business docketed with the Supreme Court is disposed of summarily by *per curiam* opinion or by order. Most of the examples above are of the latter type. When one examines the form and content of *per curiam* opinions and summary orders, one can easily form the impression that the Justices are trying to be of as little help as possible to inferior judges. The standards that guide the Justices to their conclusions are rarely revealed to the lower courts for their instruction and benefit.

To argue that the Court is interested only in broad public-law questions of national consequence is to ignore the facts that, on the one hand, the Justices *do* duck questions from below which by any reasonable standard meet the test of public significance, while on the other they accept and decide some that affect virtually no one but the immediate parties. In the end, of course, the Justices determine the questions they will answer according to whatever standards they see fit to apply. The process by which review of lower-court decisions is controlled can be judged only by its results.

The summary treatment given many lower-court decisions by the Supreme Court has evoked criticism from some of its members. Justice Black, with the support of Justices Harlan and Stewart, asserted that reversal of a lower-court decision

by a cryptic, uninformative *per curiam* order is no way, I think, for this Court to decide a case involving as this one does a State's power to make it an offense for people to obstruct public streets and highways and to block ingress and egress to and from its public buildings and property. . . . The summary disposition the Court makes of this case fails properly to enlighten state or federal courts or the people who deserve to know what are the rights of the people, the rights of affected groups, the rights of the Federal Government, and the rights of the States in this field of activity which encompasses some of the most burning, pressing, and important issues of our time. . . . These issues are of such great importance that I am of the opinion that before this Court relegates the States to the position of mere onlookers in struggles over their streets and the accesses to their public buildings, this Court should at least write an opinion making clear to the States and interested people the bounds between what they can do in this field and what they cannot. Today's esoteric and more or less mysterious *per curium* order gives no such information.[45]

The Court's typical use of a *per curiam* opinion to vacate the judgment of a District Court is illustrated by the following majority statement employed in *Cameron* v. *Johnson*:

> The motion for leave to proceed *in forma pauperis* is granted. The judgment is vacated and the cause remanded for reconsideration in light of *Dombrowski* v. *Pfister*, 380 U. S. 479. On remand, the District Court should first consider whether 28 U. S. C. § 2283 (1958 ed.) bars a federal injunction in this case, see 380 U. S., at 484, n. 2. If § 2283 is not a bar, the court should then determine whether relief is proper in light of the criteria set forth in *Dombrowski*.[46]

Once taken, summary disposition can have a heavy impact upon the fate of the litigation. By summary orders the Court negates proceedings of lower courts without any showing that a litigant was in some way adversely affected and entitled to relief. Its use of such terse and unrevealing language as that quoted above, although admittedly apt to be more revealing to a judge than it appears on its face to be, sometimes makes it impossible for lower judges to know what the Court has ruled or which of the two or more contentions urged upon it in review induced it to reverse or to affirm. Indeed, in *Cameron* v. *Johnson*, Justices Black, White, Stewart, and Harlan made it clear that they did not understand *Dombrowski* v. *Pfister*, which the district judge was directed to apply on remand, to mean the same thing as did the majority. But from the majority statement, quoted here in full, who can say with any assurance what the majority took it to mean? Further, the nature and the purpose of the writ of certiorari would seem to preclude the Court's ruling upon important questions of public law before deciding to grant the review sought by the writ; yet summary reversals of lower-

---

45. Justice Black dissenting in *Cameron* v. *Johnson*, 381 U.S. 741, 742–743 (1965). Justice Goldberg also protested against summary *affirmance* on appeal in the *Kennecott Company* case, 381 U.S. 414 (1964).

46. 381 U.S. 741, 742, 743 (1965).

court decisions in situations presenting constitutional attacks are common. Although a district and appellate tribunal may have reached the same conclusion, the Court on occasion, without opposing brief or oral argument, has nevertheless summarily reversed the lower courts. Such conclusions must approximate the ambiguity of Delphic oracular pronouncements.

The practice of summary disposition enables the Court to grant or withhold the relief sought and at the same time to control the lower courts. It has become the most important means by which the Court disposes of business brought to it. The use of summary disposition extends to a wide range of cases, including such diverse subject matter as denaturalization, obscenity, procedural rules, the Jones Merchant Seaman's Act, the Federal Employer's Liability Act, and habeas corpus proceedings in federal courts seeking to vacate state-court sentences. Edward Brown has criticized the Court's summary reversal of lower-court determinations, pointing out that this practice can cut off further consideration below of relevant (and possibly controlling) points which have been left open and undecided by the lower court.[47]

The Court purports to employ summary disposition only in instances of "clearly erroneous" conclusions below, but how can such conclusions be identified except upon adequate inquiry into the entire situation? Moreover, if the Justices are divided, can it be said that the courts below were "clearly" in error? Again, if the questions are of sufficient merit and importance for the Supreme Court of the United States to answer at all, are they not too important for it to answer except after full consideration of the briefs, record, and oral argument? The Court is of course caught in the pressure of time, and the temptation to resort to summary disposition must be great. Nevertheless, summary disposition greatly increases the power of the High Court over the inferior tribunals, and it does not aid their intelligent resolution of issues under the High Court's guidance.

Summary disposition does offer one possibly redeeming feature. Its use can enhance the appearance that the Court is united in its tests with lower tribunals. Because no reasoned statement is set out in support of the conclusions they have reached, it is not necessary for the Justices to find common

47. See E. Brown, foreword to "The Supreme Court: 1957 Term," 72 *Harvard Law Review* 77 (1958).

ground upon which to take a public stand. Use of the *per curiam* opinion or the summary order enables the Justices to render decisions for which they are largely able to escape criticism. Either can be used to avoid involvement in a potential or developed issue of substantive law. The bluntness of summary disposition conveys to litigants, counsel, and lower courts that a matter previously considered has been disposed of with finality. Summary disposition has a forceful and assertive character which has led two commentators to note that increasingly the Supreme Court's output has incorporated "the sweeping dogmatic statement," set forth little or no reasoning to support the results it has reached, and included per curiam orders that do not provide adequate linkage between the precedents relied upon and cited and the results decreed.[48]

Since most categories of summary disposition have force as precedent, the real problem for lower courts is what meaning to attribute to a particular instance of its use. Sometimes the High Court has used summary disposition to put forth a rule of law, and then it has confounded the lower tribunals by citing as authority for its action cases that bear only a slight resemblance to the one at hand, or ones that do not provide reasoning clearly applicable to the instant situation, or ones that can be interpreted more than one way. But lower courts that have been confronted by such circumstances when a case came back on remand have sometimes been able to use the resulting uncertainty to their own advantage. Withal, however, the pressures of caseload and time that compel use of summary procedures do nothing to promote smoothly working, harmonious, and coordinated relationships between the Supreme Court and the inferior tribunals.

THE INFLUENCE OF LITERARY STYLE

Not only may the form of the High Court's opinions and orders affect its relations with courts below; so also may their literary style. Many opinions appear to be much longer than needed. Among the members of the Court there is great variation

48. A. M. Bickel and H. H. Wellington, "Legislative Purpose and the Judicial Process: The Lincoln Mills Case," 71 *Harvard Law Review* 1 (1957), at p. 3. For an extended discussion of the Court's use of memorandum opinions see Note, "Supreme Court Per Curiam Practice: A Critique," 69 *Harvard Law Review* 707 (1956).

in style and writing ability, so some bear a larger share of blame than others. But too often obscure language, divergent reasoning in support of the same conclusion, unnecessary exhibitions of learning that produce endless pages of details, gossamer distinctions, and wire-drawn conclusions are set out to guide the lower tribunals. Of course, hasty writing is partly caused by the quantity of litigation that presses upon the High Court. Prof. John P. Frank has concluded that the Court is more important as the "great educator of the American scene" than it is as chief judicial "arbitrator." Given the Court's workload, its significant contribution, he states, is found to lie more in what it can induce other parties to decide than in the decisions it makes, and to illustrate his point he cites the general stimulus to lower-court action produced by a few desegregation cases involving a few elementary school children.[49]

The consequences of the literary styles that find their way into the Justices' opinions are numerous and vexing. Although legal writing is not governed by quite the same rules of composition as fine literature, to be useful, the product should possess instructive merit and a compelling force of logical reasoning tempered by practicality and supported by legal authorities. However, when clarity and directness of reasoning are displaced by discursiveness, question-begging, irrelevancies, and the like, the judges below may be at least partially excused if they look elsewhere for guidance.

Some ambiguity is inherent in the collegial character of the Court's opinions. If all Justices hear a case, at least five must be able to find a common ground of law upon which they can stand to deliver a decision. The process of achieving agreement necessitates considerable blending of viewpoints and blunting of personal convictions, with the result that the ambiguities of a particular opinion may reflect the inability of a majority precisely to define a mutually agreeable basis of decision. Ambiguity may also be used intentionally to leave room for future doctrinal maneuvering, or to pass maximum latitude for discretionary action along to the lower tribunals. Inferior judges may thus find refuge in multiple opinions, dissents, and ambiguities of the Justices.

Nevertheless, most weaknesses of Supreme Court prose are probably not intentional. The incorporation of nonessential

49. *Marble Palace* (Knopf, 1956), p. 290. Ch. 7 contains an interesting analysis of the literary qualities of Supreme Court writings.

material into an opinion may becloud the real basis of decision in a haze of dicta, so that a lower-court judge may have difficulty in identifying and adhering conscientiously to the High Court's direction. Moreover, only the Justices can say what part of today's opinion will be regarded in the future as dicta. The judge below may also find that an opinion setting out a main cord of legal reasoning contains one or more subordinate principles running through it.

Admittedly, in order to educate, lead the lower courts, institute optimum uniformity in national law, and harmonize decisions of courts below, the Supreme Court must paint with sweeping strokes on a wide canvas. Reciprocally, the inferior tribunals are largely left free to adapt general principles embodying national interests to particular disputes involving public or private concerns.

Whether the Justices write in lucid prose or with rigorous logic and extensive citations, a price is paid. The greater the explicitness and the more fine-spun the distinctions, the easier it becomes for lower-court judges to get around what their judicial superior has said. On the other hand, a lower-court judge seeking to derive a clear rule for unmistakable guidance from an opinion of the High Court probably needs logorrhea, bombast, or ponderous citation of authorities less than he needs a statement couched in clear, precise, straightforword prose setting forth the guiding principle of the case. Gratuitous display of judicial erudition is unlikely to further smooth operating relations or integration of the judicial system under the leadership, guidance, and control of the Supreme Court.

CONCLUSION

There can be no doubt that the uniqueness, prestige, and position of the Supreme Court in the constitutional judicial system lend it a powerful centralizing influence. These qualities unquestionably facilitate its exercise of control by informal influence and leadership rather than by formal statutory authority, rule-making powers, and appellate procedures. The mere fact that the Court is the highest tribunal in the nation eases its tasks of coordination, direction, and control within the federal judicial system. Whereas the Court ordinarily moves with firm popular support, any opposition that its activities generate among the inferior tribunals will probably be widely scattered.

Good judicial discipline is essential to smooth intercourt relations. A primary function of the Supreme Court is to promote an effective and expeditious administration of judicial business by the lower tribunals of the federal court system. For their part, the lesser tribunals should operate so that no color of disrepute is likely to dilute public esteem for, or confidence in, the judicial system as a whole. Failure to attain reciprocity of tolerance and respect can precipitate on a controversial subject about which convictions run deep a wave of "wrong" decisions and appeals from below sufficient to disrupt, even to endanger, the established pattern of things. Then the usual tools, methods, and procedures of the judicial process, which are based upon the existence of good discipline within the court structure, would probably be rendered inadequate to the task. They would, temporarily at least, cease to perform their function of bringing about compliance with the sense and language of the Supreme Court. Under the resulting strains, smooth intercourt relations would be endangered, and the rights of litigants and the judicial system would thereby suffer from the resulting non-compliance, friction, and uncertainty.

Index

Index